BUTTERMILK & BOURBON

NEW ORLEANS RECIPES WITH A MODERN FLAIR

JASON SANTOS

chef & owner of boston's buttermilk & bourbon

PAGE STREET
PUBLISHING CO.

First published in 2019 by

Page Street Publishing Co.

27 Congress Street, Suite 105

Salem, MA 01970

www.pagestreetpublishing.com

Distributed by Macmillan, sales in Canada by The Canadian Manda Group.

23   22   21   20   19   1   2   3   4   5

ISBN-13: 978-1-62414-629-9

ISBN-10: 1-62414-629-5

Library of Congress Control Number: 2018943559

Cover and book design by Sara Pollard for Page Street Publishing Co.

Photography by Ken Goodman

Printed and bound in China

CONTENTS

PREAMBLE

I cannot tell you how many times I get the question, "When did you know you wanted to be a chef?" I actually don't really have an "aha" answer to that question, because I honestly cannot remember when I have ever not wanted to be a chef. I know people in their 40s that still don't know what they want to be when they grow up. I am very lucky to have known at a very young age. I often joke that I came out of the womb making aioli, but I do remember being a child watching *Yan Can Cook*, Julia Child and *The Frugal Gourmet* and then going into my grandmother's kitchen and adding spices to her spaghetti sauce when she wasn't looking. I even remember putting cayenne in it once and ruining it, then completely denying it—but I had to express my creativity!

I started working at a bowling alley snack bar in my teens, and that is where, ironically, I really fell in love with preparing food. Although that food was mostly frozen and mediocre, I got a lot of satisfaction being in a kitchen, and it made me passionate about being around food. I knew then that I had to go to culinary school and become a chef.

Flash forward 20 years: My now wife surprised me with a birthday trip to New Orleans a few years back, and it literally changed my life. I love everything about that city: the food, the people and the passion! It was that trip—and the many, many return trips—that led me to open my passion project, Buttermilk & Bourbon.

When I opened the restaurant, there wasn't really anything like it in Boston. It definitely was a leap of faith, but it totally paid off. Buttermilk & Bourbon has become very successful and has led me to use the same business model in my other restaurants. So what accounts for the success? I think the food is both authentic in flavor and also prepared in inventive, surprising ways. The space was designed by Erica Diskin and is so creative—each room has its own identity and plenty of cool details that just make you want to whip out your camera and take photos. I think the attention to detail and all the fun touches like getting your check attached to a voodoo doll with blue hair or having your drink come out smoking with liquid nitrogen really grab your attention. We have an amazing patio and raw bar as well, which just creates a fun environment where people enjoy spending time together.

I also have done a lot of TV in my day, which has actually really taught me a lot about food, restaurants and business. From being the runner-up on *Hell's Kitchen* and getting to cook next to Michelin-starred chef Gordon Ramsay every day to being on the road with Jon Taffer as one of his experts helping failing bars and restaurants on *Bar Rescue*, I think seeing what not to do as a chef or restaurateur has actually helped spur me to be more creative in my thinking.

All of the above have helped me create this cookbook. People ask me why I would be willing to give away all my recipes so easily. The answer is also very easy . . . I wrote these recipes, I stand by these recipes, I love this food and I literally can't think of one person I know that loves what they do more than me. I want you to be a part of that love. I want you to make these recipes at home and see why Buttermilk & Bourbon has been a hit since day one. So here we go . . .

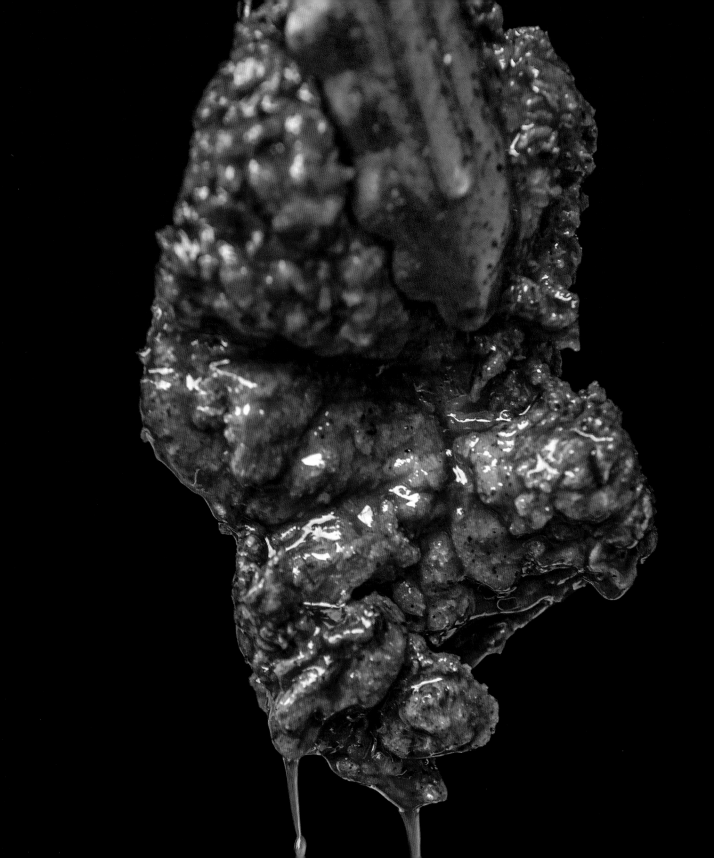

BUTTERMILK SIGNATURES

Signatures—whether it's a signature basketball dunk, wrestling move or even a movie catchphrase—are the things you really remember. Strong signature moves or dishes are important for a chef and a restaurant because they're what you become known for. As a chef, however, you don't always get to choose what your signatures are—the guests do! Signatures are the dishes people talk about or the ones that make them return. And so for you, in this chapter, I have a year's worth of the things people couldn't help but come back for.

Literally the Best Fried Chicken wings in the History of chicken

About 15 years ago, I had fried chicken at my friend Chef Jasper White's restaurant The Summer Shack, and it was the best I have ever had by a landslide. He told me a couple of things about the marinade and the cooking, but he said the rest was a secret. I never forgot that while I was perfecting my own recipe. Now the secret recipe is passed down to you, and you get the whole thing. So here it is . . . I present to you the best fried chicken wings EVER. Serve them tossed with Sweet and Spicy Glaze (page 158), dipped into White BBQ Sauce (page 151), drizzled with Jalapeño BBQ Syrup (page 158) or tossed with Nashville Hot Spice (page 157).

◆ **Makes 24 Wings** ◆

1 dozen chicken wings, split and wing tips removed

8 cups (2 L) cooking fat (canola oil, lard, duck fat, etc.)

2 cups (475 ml) Buttermilk Marinade (page 163)

4 cups (500 g) Signature Fry Dredge (page 164)

Salt and pepper, to taste

Preheat the oven to 300°F (149°C). Place the wings in a deep pan and cover with canola oil or other cooking fat. Place in the oven for 1 hour. Remove the wings from the fat (reserve the fat for your next batch) and soak the chicken wings in the Buttermilk Marinade in the refrigerator for a minimum of 4 hours, preferably overnight.

Once ready to cook, heat the cooking fat to 350°F (177°C) in either a medium pot or a cast-iron pan. Remove the chicken from the marinade, discarding the marinade, and toss the chicken in the fry dredge until completely coated. Shake off excess dredge. Carefully add the chicken to the hot fat and cook for 10 to 12 minutes, until golden brown. When done, season with salt and pepper and eat as is or toss with your favorite sauce.

BUTTERMILK & BOURBON'S HONEY-GLAZED BISCUITS

Every Southern grandmother thinks that her biscuit recipe is the best! Well I assure you, in this case I am THE Southern grandma. I tested this recipe almost every day for a year until this was the best biscuit I had ever eaten.

◆━━ **MAKES 12 LARGE BISCUITS** ━━◆

1 cup (227 g) unsalted butter, melted

5 cups (710 g) self-rising flour, plus extra for shaping

1 cup (227 g) chilled unsalted butter, cut into ¼-inch (6-mm) pieces

1 cup (227 g) chilled unsalted butter, cut into ½-inch (12-mm) pieces

3 cups (710 ml) full-fat ice-cold buttermilk

Infused Honey (page 169), for serving

Large flaked sea salt, to taste

Pimento Cheese (page 170) and/or Smoked Cinnamon Butter (page 175), for serving

Preheat the oven to 375°F (191°C). Using a 10 x 12-inch (25 x 30–cm) baking pan that is 2 inches (5 cm) deep, add the melted butter and evenly distribute, then set aside.

Sift the flour into a mixing bowl, then add the ¼-inch (6-mm) butter cubes and, using your fingers, snap the butter into the flour until the mixture is crumbly. Then add the ½-inch (12-mm) butter cubes and snap until nothing bigger than a bean remains. Do not take more than 5 minutes or the butter will start to melt. Add the cold buttermilk and mix gently until the dough just barely forms, then turn the mixture onto a floured surface and pat and shape the dough into a ¾-inch (18-mm) thick sheet (do not overmix).

Using a flour-dusted 3-inch (8-cm) ring mold, cut the biscuits and place in the baking pan. Bake for 30 to 40 minutes depending on how brown you like the top to be. When done, brush with warm Infused Honey of your choice and sprinkle with the flaked sea salt. Serve warm with Pimento Cheese and Smoked Cinnamon Butter.

Chicken & Waffle Tacos

This is one of the coolest presentations you will find. Is it a taco or is it chicken and waffles? Well, it's both. It's obviously at heart some good Southern chicken and waffles but with a Latin twist for some flair and funk. We actually serve this at my Mexican restaurant, but it's a nod to the good old South.

◆ ❲ Makes 6 servings ❳ ◆

Chicken

8 large boneless, skinless chicken thighs, trimmed of excess fat and cut in half the long way

2 cups (475 ml) Buttermilk Marinade (page 163)

4 cups (500 g) Signature Fry Dredge (page 164)

8 cups (2 L) canola oil or other fat, for frying

Salt and pepper, to taste

Lime Syrup

2 cups (475 ml) agave syrup

1 tbsp (16 g) Asian chili paste (sambal oelek)

Zest and juice of 2 limes

½ tsp smoked salt

Watermelon Pico de Gallo

2 cups (304 g) diced watermelon

¼ cup (40 g) minced red onion

2 tbsp (30 ml) lime juice

2 tbsp (2 g) minced cilantro

1 tsp minced jalapeño

Salt and pepper, to taste

Once the chicken is cut, soak the pieces in the Buttermilk Marinade in the refrigerator for a minimum of 4 hours but preferably overnight. Once ready to cook, remove the chicken from the marinade and toss in the fry dredge until completely coated. In either a medium pot or a cast-iron pan, heat the canola oil to 350°F (177°C). Carefully add the chicken to the hot oil and cook for 10 to 12 minutes, until golden brown. When done remove the chicken from the oil and season with salt and pepper.

For the lime syrup, bring the agave syrup to a boil on the stovetop. Remove the pan from the heat and add the chili paste, lime zest and juice and smoked salt. Keep warm.

For the watermelon pico de gallo, combine the diced watermelon, red onion, lime juice, cilantro and jalapeño and season with salt and pepper to taste.

(continued)

Chicken & Waffle Tacos (Cont.)

Avocado Butter

½ cup (115 g) fresh avocado pulp

1 tbsp (15 ml) lime juice

1 clove garlic, minced

½ tsp ground cumin

½ cup (115 g) unsalted butter, softened

Salt and pepper, to taste

Waffle Batter

2 cups (240 g) all-purpose flour

1 cup (120 g) blue cornmeal

6 tbsp (75 g) sugar

1 tbsp (14 g) baking powder

½ tsp salt

2 tbsp (30 ml) bourbon

1 cup (237 ml) milk

1 cup (237 ml) buttermilk

4 eggs

6 tbsp (85 g) unsalted butter, melted

Cilantro sprigs, for garnish

Lime wedges, for serving

For the avocado butter, puree the avocado pulp, lime juice, garlic and cumin in a food processor until smooth. Add the butter and puree to combine. Season with salt and pepper. This will keep in the refrigerator for a week, or you can freeze it until you are ready to use.

For the waffles, preheat the waffle iron according to the manufacturer's settings. Sift together the flour, blue cornmeal, sugar, baking powder and salt in a large bowl. In a separate bowl, whisk together the bourbon, milk, buttermilk and eggs. Pour the wet ingredients into the dry ingredients and stir until halfway combined. Pour in the melted butter and continue mixing very gently until combined. Scoop the batter into the preheated waffle iron in batches and cook according to the manufacturer's directions, or until the waffles are deep golden and crisp.

Remove the waffle from the iron, fold it and place in a taco stand. Top with 2 strips of fried chicken and pico de gallo. Garnish with cilantro and serve with lime wedges, lime syrup and avocado butter.

10-Way Cut
Nashville Fried Chicken

OMG this is hot! BUT it has so much zip it's worth the burn. You can obviously use less spice to tone it down, but I think if you are going to do it, do it right! Traditionally, once cooked, the chicken gets tossed in some additional frying oil then spiced in order to almost create a paste, and that is what gives the chicken its beautiful fiery red color. I know tossing something that was just fried in more fat seems crazy and a bit of overkill, but that is the key. And MY secret is I use rendered pork fat instead of frying oil. It gives it so much added flavor and richness. I promise that if you don't like my version better, especially with pickled tomatoes instead of basic pickle chips, I will personally come and eat the rest of it for you. It hurts so good!

Serves 2 to 4

Green Tomato Relish

1 cup (237 ml) water

1 cup (237 ml) white vinegar

¼ cup (50 g) sugar

¼ cup (75 g) salt

¼ cup (25 g) minced scallions

1 clove garlic, minced

1 jalapeño, minced

3 medium-size green tomatoes, diced

1 bay leaf

1 tsp mustard seed

½ tsp smoked paprika

1 tsp ground turmeric

¼ tsp crab boil spice seasoning (I prefer Zatarain's)

½ tsp red pepper flakes

To make the relish, bring the water, vinegar, sugar and salt to a boil in a saucepan over medium heat. Place the scallions, garlic, jalapeño, green tomatoes, bay leaf, mustard seed, smoked paprika, turmeric, crab boil seasoning and red pepper flakes in a bowl. Pour the hot liquid over the ingredients in the bowl and let the mixture sit in the refrigerator overnight. This will last about 10 days in your refrigerator.

To break down your chicken into 10 pieces, first you name your chicken. I will name mine Frank.

1. With Frank breast up, cut Frank's leg away from his body.

2. Turn Frank on his side. Bend each of Frank's legs back until his thigh bone pops out of its socket. Cut through the joint, then cut through the skin and remove completely.

3. With Frank on his side, pull each of his wings away from his body. Cut through the joint and remove the wing.

4. Lift up Frank and cut downward through his rib cage and then his shoulder joints to separate the breast from the back. Save the backbone for stock.

5. Place Frank's breast skin-side down. Cut the center bone to separate into 2 pieces.

(continued)

Chicken

1 whole chicken, washed with cold water and dried with paper towels

2 cups (475 ml) Buttermilk Marinade (page 163)

4 cups (500 g) Signature Fry Dredge (page 164)

8 cups (2 L) canola oil, for frying

¼ cup (59 ml) warm rendered pork fat (aka lard)

2 tbsp (14 g) or more Nashville Hot Spice (page 157)

Salt and pepper, to taste

6. To cut Frank's breast halves into quarters, turn each piece skin-side up and cut in half diagonally through the bone.

7. To divide Frank's legs, turn each leg skin-side down and cut through the joints (along the white fat line) to separate the thigh from the drumstick.

8. If you did this right, you'll end up with Frank cut into 10 pieces. If you have 11, something went horribly wrong.

Once the chicken is cut, soak it in the Buttermilk Marinade in the refrigerator for a minimum of 4 hours but preferably overnight. Once ready to cook, remove the chicken from the marinade, discarding the marinade, and toss the chicken in the fry dredge until it is completely coated.

In either a medium pot or a cast-iron pan, heat the canola oil to 330°F (166°C). Carefully add the chicken to the hot oil and cook for 10 to 12 minutes, until golden brown. When done, remove the chicken from the oil and place in a large mixing bowl. Toss the chicken with the pork fat and dust with the Nashville Hot Spice until it is well coated (the more you add, the hotter it gets). Season with salt and pepper and top with the relish.

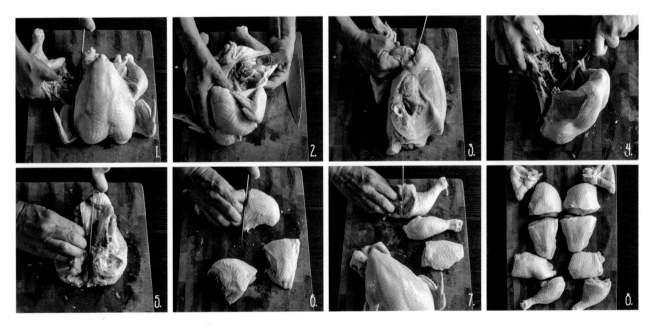

Flamin' Hot Cheeto Mac & Cheese

I believe the title speaks for itself. Not much to say about this one except trust me and—oh, yeah—this is the #1 selling dish in my restaurant.

◆———— SERVES 4 ————◆

4 tbsp (56 g) unsalted butter, divided

1 cup (225 g) meat scraps, diced (bacon, andouille, tasso, pork belly, ham, etc.)

½ cup (50 g) diced celery

¾ cup (120 g) diced shallots

1 tbsp (8 g) minced garlic

1 tbsp (16 g) tomato paste

1 cup (237 ml) white wine

2 bay leaves

1 tbsp (3 g) fresh thyme, chopped

8 oz (227 g) cream cheese

1 cup (237 ml) heavy cream

1 cup (237 ml) half & half

½ cup (50 g) grated Parmesan cheese

½ cup (56 g) shredded fontina

½ cup (56 g) shredded yellow cheddar

½ cup (56 g) shredded gouda

½ lb (227 g) campanelle pasta, cooked

Salt and pepper, to taste

1 cup (45 g) spicy cheese puffs (I like Flamin' Hot Cheetos), slightly crushed

¼ cup (12 g) minced chives

½ cup (22 g) spicy cheese puffs, whole

Preheat the oven to 400°F (204°C). In a heavy-bottomed pot, melt 2 tablespoons (28 g) of the butter and sauté the meat scraps until lightly browned, about 3 to 5 minutes. Remove the meat, reserving the fat. Then add the celery, shallots and garlic and cook until soft, about 3 to 5 minutes. Add the tomato paste and cook for another 3 minutes to incorporate. Deglaze with the wine and reduce by half, about 10 minutes. Add the bay leaves, thyme, cream cheese, heavy cream and half & half. Bring to a simmer for 10 minutes. Add the Parmesan, fontina, cheddar and gouda and simmer for 10 more minutes. Remove the bay leaves and puree the entire mixture with a stick blender (or in batches using a regular blender/food processor). Add the meat scraps back to the pot.

Combine the sauce with the cooked pasta and season with salt and pepper.

Divide the mixture into 4 casserole dishes. Melt the remaining 2 tablespoons (28 g) of butter and combine with the crushed Cheetos, and scatter on top of the pasta mixture. Bake for about 7 minutes or until bubbly. Garnish with chives and the whole Cheetos.

NOTE: If you are making this ahead of time, wait to combine the sauce with the macaroni until you are ready to bake the entire dish. Otherwise, the sauce will get absorbed into the pasta and you will lose the wonderful creamy sauciness of the dish.

PORK BELLY CRACKLINGS WITH CHEDDAR SALT

When we first opened we were always running out of this dish, until one day I realized that the cooks were eating more than we were actually selling. Well, I had to lead by example on this one, so instead of stopping them, we just ramped up production to feed our cravings.

◆ SERVES 6 AS A SNACK ◆

PORK BELLY

8 cups (2 L) House Brine (page 152)

2-lb (907-g) slab meaty pork belly, skin removed

About 6 cups (1.4 L) fat (lard, blended oil, duck fat, etc.)

CHEDDAR SALT

2 bags powdered cheese mix from boxes of mac and cheese

1 tsp crab boil spice mix (I prefer Zatarain's)

1 tbsp (17 g) salt

1 tsp House Cajun Spice (page 155)

Canola oil, for frying

Pour the brine into a container large enough to hold the pork belly and add the pork. Refrigerate overnight. Remove the pork belly and rinse under cold water. Pat dry. Preheat the oven to 275°F (135°C). Choose an ovenproof pan that is only slightly larger than the pork belly and has a lid; the pot should be deep enough that the pork will be submerged. Put the pork belly in the pan and cover with the fat. The fat should cover the pork by ½ to ¾ inch (1.3 to 1.9 cm).

Transfer to the oven, and cook until the pork is tender; this will probably take 4 hours or more, but start checking after 3 hours. Remove the pan from the oven and let the pork cool to room temperature. It can simply be refrigerated in its fat for up to 1 week, or you can use it once it's cold.

To make the cheddar salt, combine the cheese mix, crab boil spice, salt and Cajun spice and mix.

Remove the pork from the fat (reserve the fat for later use) and cut into medium-size chunks. In a pot or cast-iron pan, heat 2 inches (5 cm) of canola oil to 350°F (177°C). Line a plate with a paper towel. Put the pieces of belly in the oil and cook until crispy but not dried out, about 5 minutes. Season liberally with cheddar salt and serve with any of the sauces from the Brines, Rubs, Seasonings & Marinades chapter (page 149).

NOTE: Blended oil is something I buy. Essentially it is a 90/10 canola to extra-virgin olive oil mix.

New Orleans BBQ Shrimp With Jalapeño Grits

This recipe makes the top 5 of all time in my opinion. It's spicy, salty, creamy and vinegary all in one bite. We tried to take this off the menu at the restaurant and I received sternly worded letters from guests asking me why I would do such a thing. It is back on the menu and will probably never leave.

Serves 4 as an appetizer

BBQ Base

1 tbsp (15 ml) blended oil

Reserved shrimp shells

2 cloves garlic, roughly chopped

2 lemons, peeled

½ cup (118 ml) Worcestershire sauce

½ cup (118 ml) hot sauce

Jalapeño Grits

2 tsp (9 g) butter

1 tsp blended oil

1 jalapeño, small diced

1 cup (150 g) diced onion

4 cups (1 L) chicken stock

3 cups (710 ml) water

2 cups (340 g) stone-ground grits

8 oz (227 g) cream cheese

Salt and pepper, to taste

Shrimp

1 lb (454 g) shrimp, peeled and deveined, reserve shells

2 tsp (5 g) House Cajun Spice (page 155)

1 tbsp (15 ml) blended oil

¼ cup (59 ml) of your favorite beer

2 tbsp (28 g) cold unsalted butter, cubed

Grilled bread, for serving (optional)

For the BBQ base, place the oil in a small saucepan over medium-high heat. Add the reserved shrimp shells and the garlic, stirring frequently until the shells are golden brown, about 4 minutes. Add the lemons, Worcestershire and hot sauce. Lower the heat to medium and let simmer until reduced by half, about 4 to 6 minutes. Strain and set the sauce aside. This can be made a day ahead.

For the grits, heat the butter and oil in a pan and add the jalapeño and onion. Cook until softened, 5 minutes or so. Pour in the chicken stock and water. Stir, and then bring to a boil. Whisk in the grits, then reduce the heat to low, cover and cook for 30 to 40 minutes, stirring occasionally. Add the cream cheese. Stir and cook until the grits are tender, another 20 to 30 minutes. At any time, add more stock if the grits look like they need more cooking liquid. Remove the grits from the heat and season with salt and pepper.

For the shrimp, toss the peeled shrimp with the House Cajun Spice, then add the blended oil to a medium-size sauté pan over high heat. Add the shrimp and sear 1 minute per side, then add the beer, stir, let reduce for 1 minute and reduce the heat to medium. Add the BBQ base and let it reduce for 3 minutes. Turn the heat off and swirl in the cold butter. Serve immediately over jalapeño grits with some grilled bread.

NOTE: For me, hot sauce is always Crystal brand hot sauce. I just think it is the best. Not too hot with tons of flavor. You can use Frank's as well. But not Tabasco or sriracha. They are very different.

MUST-HAVE MEATS & SAUCES

Cooking meat can be stressful. There are so many things that can go wrong: undercooked, overcooked, too dry, too charred, not charred enough, not seasoned right, etc. It's the one thing that I think most home cooks tend to screw up. I intentionally picked recipes that have taken me many tries to perfect, but, lucky for you, I have taken all the guesswork out of them. I have given you some of my greats, as they say, using lots of key Southern ingredients like andouille and pork ribs. You can now re-create these at home, and I'm giving you permission to completely take credit for them—I mean, I would!

ANDOUILLE SAUSAGE

There is something that I really like about andouille sausage. It has more heat and spice than other types and just looks better. This is a great recipe that you can form into patties for brunch, use in place of the beef in Blackened Prime Burger Sliders (page 38), stuff into casings for the grill or just keep in the freezer when you need to up your flavor game.

◆━━━❨ MAKES ABOUT 6 CUPS (1½ KG) ❩━━━◆

3 lbs (1.3 kg) boneless pork butt, ½-inch (12-mm) dice

¼ cup (34 g) garlic cloves

¼ cup (31 g) House Cajun Spice (page 155)

2 tbsp (14 g) smoked paprika

2 tsp (5 g) black pepper

2 tsp (5 g) Korean chili powder

4 tsp (24 g) salt

1 tsp filé powder

1 tsp red pepper flakes

1 tsp garlic powder

1 tsp ground cumin

1 tsp blended cooking oil

Sausage casings (optional)

Combine the pork, garlic, House Cajun Spice, paprika, black pepper, chili powder, salt, filé powder, red pepper flakes, garlic powder and cumin in a large bowl and mix well. Pass through a food grinder fitted with a coarse die. Alternately, transfer in 2 batches to a food processor and process until finely ground. Transfer to a large bowl, cover tightly with plastic wrap and refrigerate overnight.

To test the spice level, heat 1 teaspoon of oil in a small skillet, and cook 1 tablespoon (15 g) of the mixture. Adjust the seasoning to taste. The sausage meat is now ready to be used for crumbles, patties or just an ingredient. Or, you can use the sausage attachment on a mixer to stuff the meat into the casings. Twist and tie off the casing to make 4-inch (10-cm) sausages. Preheat a home smoker to 250°F (121°C), then smoke the sausage for 1½ hours.

Grilled Baby Back Ribs

I know wrapping something in plastic and then putting it into the oven might sound crazy, but trust me on this one. Wrapping these ribs in plastic wrap keeps all the moisture inside, almost steaming the ribs. I personally promise that this is the most tender and moist thing you will ever eat.

Serves 1 if you're me or 4 if you're lame

Hot Cherry Peppers

1 lb (454 g) fresh hot cherry peppers

2 tbsp + 1 cup (266 ml) extra-virgin olive oil, divided

1 cup (237 ml) water

1 cup (237 ml) cider vinegar

2 tbsp (35 g) salt

4 cloves garlic, minced

½ tsp red pepper flakes

½ tsp black pepper

Ribs

1 rack baby back ribs

1 cup (165 g) AKA Rub (page 154)

Salt and pepper, to taste

1 cup (237 ml) or more Carolina Gold Sauce (page 162)

¼ cup (25 g) thinly sliced scallions

1 cup (104 g) pickled hot cherry peppers

For the peppers, preheat a grill. Toss the peppers in 2 tablespoons (30 ml) of the oil and grill just until charred but still kind of raw, a few minutes. Remove from the grill and let come to room temperature. Remove the stems and quarter the peppers. Bring the water, vinegar, salt, garlic, red pepper flakes and black pepper to a boil and pour over the peppers. Let sit in the refrigerator for 3 days, then remove the peppers from the brine and toss with the remaining cup (237 ml) of extra-virgin olive oil. These will keep for a couple of weeks refrigerated.

For the ribs, preheat the oven to 275°F (135°C). Rub the rack of ribs liberally with AKA Rub and then season with salt and pepper. Wrap the ribs in plastic wrap, then wrap in aluminum foil and place on a baking sheet. Cook for 3 hours, until the meat is very tender but still has a tug. Place the ribs into the refrigerator and wait patiently until the ribs are cold. This will make them easier to cut.

Cut each bone. Place the ribs on a hot grill and cook until hot with a nice crispy texture, about 3 to 5 minutes. Toss the ribs in Carolina Gold Sauce, and garnish with scallions and hot peppers. Serve immediately.

Grilled Cider-Brined Pork Tenderloin

God, I love this recipe, I mean I seriously love this recipe. I have never met or served someone who doesn't like this dish, and that is a big deal. From the sweet apple-brined pork to the tart cranberries to the creamy turnips and the peppery nasturtiums, I keep this dish in my back pocket until it's ready to be unleashed.

Serves 6

Pork Tenderloin

3 large pork tenderloins (about 2 lbs [907 g])

½ batch Apple Cider Brine (page 153)

Vegetable oil

Salt and pepper, to taste

Maple-Cranberry Glaze

2 cups (475 ml) pure Vermont maple syrup

½ cup (115 g) unsalted butter

¼ cup (40 g) minced red onion

6 cloves garlic, minced

2 cups (227 g) fresh cranberries

1 tbsp (3 g) dried thyme

2 tbsp (30 ml) white vinegar

Salt and white pepper, to taste

Buttermilk Mashed Turnips

4 lbs (1.8 kg) turnips

½ cup (118 ml) buttermilk

½ cup (118 ml) heavy cream

6 tbsp (85 g) butter

Salt and white pepper, to taste

Garnish

Nasturtium flowers

Baby arugula leaves

For the pork tenderloin, trim off any excess fat and silver skin. Add the pork to the brine and let them sit in the refrigerator overnight. Preheat your grill and brush the hot grill with vegetable oil. Remove the tenderloins from the brine, discarding the brine, and season the meat with salt and pepper, then place them in the center of the grate. Cook for 12 to 15 minutes, turning every 3 to 5 minutes, until the tenderloins reach an internal temperature of 140°F (60°C).

For the maple-cranberry glaze, combine the maple syrup, butter, onion, garlic, cranberries, thyme, vinegar, salt and pepper in a saucepan and bring to a boil. Once it has boiled and the cranberries have just split, remove it from the heat.

For the turnips, peel off the waxy skins and cut the turnips into chunks. Place them in a saucepan with water to cover. Bring to a boil and simmer, covered, until easily pierced by a paring knife, about 35 minutes. Drain.

In a separate saucepan, heat the buttermilk and heavy cream over low heat until the mixture begins to simmer. Remove from the heat. Using a potato masher, mash the turnips with the butter, then add in the liquid. Season with salt and white pepper.

To plate, slice the pork tenderloins and place atop the mashed turnips. Spoon maple-cranberry glaze over the pork and garnish with nasturtiums and/or baby arugula leaves.

Honey and Hoisin-Glazed Duck Confit

This recipe has nothing to do with New Orleans; it has, however, been my signature dish for over 15 years in my other restaurants and is probably one of my three favorite things I've ever made. I thought you should have this recipe even though the only thing this has in common with the American South is that it's from Southeast Asia. Shh, don't tell my editor this made it into the book.

◆ Serves 4 as an entree ◆

Duck Confit

4 duck leg portions with thighs attached (about 2 lbs [907 g]), excess fat trimmed and reserved

1 tbsp plus ½ tsp (21 g) salt, divided

½ tsp ground black pepper

10 cloves garlic

4 bay leaves

4 sprigs fresh thyme

1½ tsp (5 g) black peppercorns

4 cups (1 L) canola oil or rendered meat fat (duck, lard, etc.)

For the duck confit, lay the leg portions on a platter, skin-side down. Sprinkle with 1 tablespoon (17 g) of the salt and the ground black pepper. Place the garlic cloves, bay leaves and thyme sprigs on each of the 4 leg portions. Cover and refrigerate for 12 hours.

Preheat the oven to 275°F (135°C). Remove the duck from the refrigerator. Remove the garlic, bay leaves and thyme and reserve. Rinse the duck with cool water, rubbing off some of the salt and pepper. Pat dry with paper towels.

Put the reserved garlic, bay leaves, thyme and reserved fat trimming in the bottom of an enameled cast-iron pot. Sprinkle evenly with the peppercorns and remaining ½ teaspoon of salt. Lay the duck on top, skin-side down. Add the cooking fat. Cover and bake for 3 hours, or until the meat just pulls away from the bone. Remove the duck from the fat and chill. Strain the fat and reserve.

Mango Sticky Rice

2½ cups (460 g) Thai sweet sticky rice (no substitutions), soaked in water for 3 hours

1 package banana leaves, thawed

½ cup (118 ml) coconut milk

½ cup (100 g) sugar

1 tsp salt

1 ripe mango, diced

Hoisin Glaze

2 tbsp (12 g) ginger, minced

2 tbsp (17 g) garlic, minced

2 tbsp (30 ml) sesame oil

½ cup (118 ml) hoisin sauce

½ cup (118 ml) oyster sauce

½ tsp Asian chili paste (sambal oelek)

1½ tsp (7 ml) soy sauce

1½ tbsp (23 ml) honey

Plating

¼ cup plus 2 tbsp (90 ml) duck fat reserved from duck confit, divided

½ lb (227 g) bean sprouts

12 sprigs cilantro

½ cup (63 g) cashews, roasted

For the mango sticky rice, place the rice in a steamer lined with a layer of banana leaves and steam for 10 to 15 minutes. Remove the rice and put it in a bowl. Mix the coconut milk, sugar and salt in a saucepan and bring to a simmer, then remove from the heat. Add this mixture to the cooked rice and fold in the diced mango. Chill the rice until firm.

To wrap the rice, arrange 2 banana leaves in a cross. Spoon 1 cup (186 g) of the rice in the center. Fold up the top leaf like an envelope to enclose the rice. Wrap the packet with butcher's twine. Repeat with the remaining banana leaves and filling.

For the hoisin glaze, in a small pot sauté the ginger and the garlic in sesame oil until soft. Stir in the hoisin sauce, oyster sauce, chili paste, soy sauce and honey and bring to a boil. Once the sauce has come to a boil, remove from the heat until ready to serve.

To assemble, heat ¼ cup (59 ml) of the reserved fat in a large sauté pan and pan-fry the duck confit in batches until crispy on both sides, 3 to 5 minutes on each side. Resteam the rice packets for an additional 5 minutes or until soft. Remove the rice and place on a plate, then gently open the rice packets. Place the duck legs on top of the rice. Heat the remaining 2 tablespoons (30 ml) of the reserved fat and sauté the bean sprouts briefly, then add the hoisin glaze and cook just until hot. Top the duck legs with the bean sprout mixture and garnish with cilantro and cashews.

Duck Legs with Duck Fat French Fries

This is worth the work and then some. Ultimately it's all about the duck fat flavor. The fresh cut french fries are on a different level. If you are not willing to put in the work for the fries, then I will allow you to use frozen, I guess. Thankfully this is so good you could serve it on a cinder block and no one would notice.

◆ ⬟ Serves 6 ⬟ ◆

French Fries and Gravy

4 lb (1.8 kg) Idaho potatoes, skin on

¼ cup + 2 tbsp (90 ml) rendered duck fat, divided

¼ cup (40 g) minced onion

2 cloves garlic, minced

¼ cup (30 g) all-purpose flour

4 cups (1 L) crappy canned beef broth

2 tbsp (30 ml) ketchup

1 tbsp (15 ml) cider vinegar

1 tsp Worcestershire sauce

½ tsp hot sauce

½ tsp poultry seasoning

Salt and pepper, to taste

Canola oil, for frying

Plating

2 cups (126 g) cheddar cheese curds, divided

Salt and pepper, to taste

6 confit duck legs, rewarmed

½ cup (112 g) duck cracklings (see note)

2 tbsp (30 g) fresh grated horseradish

3 tbsp (9 g) minced chives

Cut the potatoes into french fry–sized matchsticks. Place them in a large bowl, cover with cold water and refrigerate for an hour or so.

Meanwhile, heat ¼ cup (60 ml) of the duck fat in a 2-quart (2-L) saucepan over medium heat. Add the onion and garlic and cook until translucent, about 2 minutes. Add the flour and cook, stirring, about 2 minutes. Add the beef broth, ketchup, vinegar, Worcestershire sauce, hot sauce, poultry seasoning, salt and pepper, and bring to a boil; cook, stirring, until thickened, about 6 minutes. Remove from the heat and keep the gravy warm.

Pour the canola oil to a depth of 3 inches (7.5 cm) in a 6-quart (6-L) Dutch oven, and heat over medium heat until a meat thermometer reads 325°F (163°C). Drain the potatoes thoroughly and dry using a towel. In small batches, add the potatoes to the hot oil and fry until tender and slightly crispy, about 4 minutes. Drain the fries and let cool for 15 minutes. Increase the oil temperature to 375°F (191°C). In small batches, return the potatoes to the oil and fry until crispy and golden brown, about 2 minutes. Remove the fries from the fryer and drain. Place the fries in a bowl and toss with the remaining 2 tablespoons (30 ml) of duck fat, half of the cheese curds and salt and pepper to taste. Divide the fries among serving bowls.

Top the fries evenly with the remaining cheese curds and meat picked from the warm duck legs. Pour the gravy over each serving of fries and garnish with crispy duck cracklings, fresh grated horseradish and chives. Serve immediately.

NOTE: **To make cracklings, remove the skins from a confit duck leg. Preheat the oven to 325°F (163°C). Spread the skins onto a flat pan like a cookie sheet, season and bake until crispy, about 20 to 25 minutes. Your time will vary depending on the amount of skin you get.**

Blackened Prime Burger Sliders

Everybody loves a good burger, and I'm no exception. I love sliders because they are just a couple of bites with no real commitment. In and out and nobody gets hurt. The muffuletta relish and the whipped goat cheese add a great contrast to this rich, fatty burger.

◆ **Makes 4 sliders** ◆

Whipped Goat Cheese

3 tbsp (45 g) goat cheese, softened

1 tbsp (15 g) cream cheese, softened

1 tsp extra-virgin olive oil

4 cloves Garlic Confit, mashed (page 185)

1 tsp Worcestershire sauce

1 tsp Asian chili paste (sambal oelek)

Salt and pepper, to taste

Muffuletta Relish

1½ tsp (4 g) pitted and roughly chopped green olives

1½ tsp (4 g) pitted and roughly chopped black olives

1 tbsp (10 g) diced red onion

1 tbsp (4 g) roughly chopped cauliflower florets

1 tbsp (10 g) diced red bell pepper

1 tbsp (8 g) diced celery

1 tbsp (8 g) diced carrot

1½ tsp (4 g) chopped capers

1 clove garlic, minced

½ tsp fresh oregano, chopped

1 tsp red wine vinegar

1 tsp lemon juice

1 tsp extra-virgin olive oil

Pinch of red pepper flakes

Salt and pepper, to taste

Sliders

1 tbsp (15 ml) blended oil

4 (3-oz [85-g]) prime-grade beef sliders

Salt and pepper, to taste

1 tbsp (7 g) House Cajun Spice (page 155)

4 potato slider buns, preferably Martin's

1 tbsp (14 g) unsalted butter

For the whipped goat cheese, whisk together the goat cheese, cream cheese, olive oil, mashed garlic, Worcestershire sauce and chili paste in a small bowl. Season to taste with salt and pepper.

For the muffuletta relish, in a small bowl, combine the green olives, black olives, red onion, cauliflower, bell pepper, celery, carrot, capers, garlic, oregano, vinegar, lemon juice, olive oil, red pepper flakes, salt and pepper and refrigerate. This will keep fresh for about a week.

For the sliders, heat a cast-iron pan over medium-high heat. Add the blended oil and season the sliders with salt, pepper and House Cajun Spice. Place the sliders in the hot pan and cook for 3 to 4 minutes. Turn the sliders over with a spatula and cook for another 3 to 4 minutes, until medium-rare, or cook longer if you prefer the sliders more well done.

Split the buns in half and, in a separate pan, toast the halves cut-side down in butter. Divide the whipped goat cheese and spread it on the 4 bottom buns. Top each bun with a slider and finish with the muffuletta relish. Cover with the top of the bun and serve hot.

Turkey and Dumplings

This is comfort food at its finest. This recipe is just a guide—you can change out the vegetables or swap out the protein, make it more wintery, make it more summery. But the moral of the story is that this recipe is extraordinary because of the way we layer and develop flavor, from slightly browning the vegetables in the butter to the choice of herbs put into the dish.

◆ ▬ Serves 6 to 8 ▬ ◆

Turkey Stew

½ cup (115 g) unsalted butter

4 cups (512 g) diced carrots

4 cups (624 g) diced celery root

4 cups (404 g) diced celery

3 cups (267 g) diced leeks

3 cups (450 g) diced onion

1 cup (87 g) diced fennel

8 cups (560 g) quartered cremini mushrooms

¼ cup (34 g) minced garlic

1 jalapeño, minced

4 bay leaves

¼ cup (10 g) chopped fresh thyme

½ cup (12 g) chopped fresh sage

3 tbsp (44 ml) vermouth

4 cups (1 L) white wine

2 cups (240 g) all-purpose flour

1 gallon (3.75 L) Smoky Ham Stock (page 178)

6 cups (750 g) shredded cooked turkey meat

½ cup (118 ml) hot sauce

½ cup (118 ml) Worcestershire sauce

2 tbsp (3 g) fresh tarragon, minced

2 tbsp (8 g) fresh parsley, minced

Salt and pepper, to taste

Dumplings

1 cup (120 g) all-purpose flour

Pinch of cayenne

Pinch of oregano

Pinch of nutmeg

1 tbsp (14 g) baking powder

Salt and pepper, to taste

1 tbsp (14 g) unsalted butter, melted

1 egg

½ cup (118 ml) buttermilk

To make the turkey stew, melt the butter over medium heat in a heavy-bottomed pot. Sauté the carrots, celery root, celery, leeks, onion, fennel, mushrooms, garlic and jalapeño until lightly browned, about 5 minutes. Add the bay leaves, thyme, sage, vermouth and white wine. Continue cooking until the liquid has reduced almost entirely. Add the flour to make a roux and cook, stirring, for 5 minutes in order to remove the flour's raw taste. Gradually stir in the ham stock and turkey meat. Simmer for 30 minutes or until the vegetables are soft but not mushy. Add the hot sauce, Worcestershire sauce, tarragon and parsley. Season with salt and pepper.

To make the dumplings, combine the flour, cayenne, oregano, nutmeg, baking powder, salt and pepper in a medium-size mixing bowl. In a separate bowl, combine the melted butter, egg and buttermilk. Add the wet ingredients to the dry ingredients and mix the two together gently, leaving some lumps.

Preheat the oven to 350°F (177°C). Pour the hot stew into a large cast-iron pan or baking dish and spoon approximately 14 to 16 tablespoons (210–240 g) of dumpling batter scattered on top of the stew. Bake for 20 to 30 minutes or until the stew is bubbly and the dumplings are cooked and golden brown. Serve immediately.

RICH & LUSH COMFORT FOODS

If I were a rapper I think Rich & Lush would be my stage name. I would rap about you getting ready for some serious comfort food coming your way. These recipes will all be about texture. From luxurious and mouthwatering like the Boiled Peanut Hummus (page 49) to luscious and decadent like the Smoked Gouda Cornbread (page 45), that is what you can expect from this chapter. Rich & Lush out! Peace!

SMOKED GOUDA CORNBREAD

The best cornbread I have ever had was made by Chef Brian Poe from Boston's Rattlesnake Bar, and he was kind enough to send me his recipe. I have changed it and adjusted it over the years, and he probably wouldn't recognize it now because of how it's evolved. But I wanted to give him a shout out for sending me in the right direction. I hope you love this recipe as much as I do.

◆━━━ SERVES 12 ━━━◆

Sriracha-Roasted Garlic Butter

¼ cup (59 ml) hot sauce

¼ cup (59 ml) sriracha

10 cloves roasted garlic

1 anchovy fillet

1 tsp salt

½ tsp red pepper flakes

¼ tsp cayenne

Zest and juice of 1 lemon

1 cup (227 g) unsalted butter, diced and softened

1 tbsp (3 g) minced chives

Smoked Gouda Cornbread

3 cups (680 g) unsalted butter, softened

2¾ cups (550 g) sugar

2 tsp (9 g) baking powder

1 tsp baking soda

1 tbsp (17 g) salt

1 tsp red pepper flakes

3 cups (342 g) masa harina, divided

12 eggs

3 cups (339 g) shredded smoked gouda

2 cups (308 g) raw corn kernels

1 cup (149 g) diced red bell pepper

2 tbsp (11 g) jalapeños, minced

4 cloves garlic, minced

For the sriracha-roasted garlic butter, place the hot sauce, sriracha, garlic, anchovy, salt, red pepper flakes, cayenne, lemon zest and juice in the bowl of a food processor and puree the mixture. Add the softened butter and puree until smooth, light and airy, about 3 to 4 minutes. Add the chives and pulse just until incorporated. Remove the butter from the bowl and spoon it onto parchment paper or plastic wrap. Roll into a log. Chill for 2 hours before serving.

For the cornbread, preheat the oven to 350°F (177°C). Cream the butter and sugar in a stand mixer with the paddle attachment for 3 minutes. Turn the mixer to low and add the baking powder, baking soda, salt, red pepper flakes and half of the masa flour. Allow to incorporate. Add eggs, one at a time, then the remaining masa flour. Add the gouda, corn, red bell pepper, jalapeños and garlic and mix just until combined.

Grease a 9 x 11-inch (23 x 28-cm) baking pan with butter or lard. Pour the cornbread mixture into the pan and cover with aluminum foil. Place the baking pan on top of a sheet tray to prevent spillage. Bake for about 30 minutes, then remove the foil and bake for 15 minutes more until firm to the touch or until a cake tester comes out clean. Remove from oven. Keep covered and let cool for 10 to 15 minutes. Remove the cornbread from the pan. Slice and serve warm with sriracha-roasted garlic butter.

Southern-Style Potato Salad

I have been using this recipe for many many years without any tweaks. The experience is so creamy and vinegary and honestly just so balanced that it makes this the most delectable potato salad ever! This potato salad is fantastic on its own, but it's often served alongside gumbo—usually more as a mash. It might sound a bit weird, but it's the law of the land—trust me.

◆ Serves 6 to 8 as a side ◆

3½ lbs (1.6 kg) red bliss potatoes, scrubbed clean

2½ cups (593 ml) mayonnaise

¼ cup (59 ml) Dijon mustard

⅓ cup (78 ml) red wine vinegar

7 hard-boiled eggs, crumbled

¼ cup (28 g) bacon bits

1 cup (100 g) minced scallions

1 cup (150 g) diced red onion

¼ cup (12 g) minced chives

Salt and pepper, to taste

Place the potatoes in a large pot of water. Bring the water to a rolling boil, then lower the heat and simmer for 15 to 20 minutes, until the potatoes are tender when pierced with a knife but not overcooked. Drain the potatoes well in a colander, then place them in the refrigerator to cool for about 20 minutes.

Meanwhile, in a small bowl, mix the mayonnaise, mustard and red wine vinegar and set aside.

When the potatoes are cool, cut them in quarters or halves, depending on their size. Place the cut potatoes in a large bowl. Add the hard-boiled eggs, bacon bits, scallions, red onion and chives. Toss well, season with salt and pepper, cover and refrigerate for a few hours to allow the flavors to blend. Serve cold or at room temperature.

Boiled Peanut Hummus

This stuff is great. I love hummus and I love that you can now get pretty much any type of hummus you want, from chocolate to chipotle. I have yet to see peanut hummus out there, but maybe after this book comes out Sabra will be giving me a call. Don't mistake this for a peanut butter–type flavor because it is not. Boiled peanuts are a Southern staple—their subtle nuttiness is scrumptious.

Serves 4 to 6

4 cups (1 kg) canned black-eyed peas, drained and rinsed

¼ batch Boiled Peanuts, Cheater's Version (page 171)

4 cloves garlic

¼ cup (59 ml) hot sauce

⅓ cup (78 ml) fresh squeezed lemon juice

¾ tsp ground cumin

½ cup (118 ml) tahini paste

¾ cup (177 ml) extra-virgin olive oil

1 cup (237 ml) water

Salt and pepper, to taste

Pepper Jack Crackers (page 65), for serving

In a food processor, combine the black-eyed peas, boiled peanuts, garlic, hot sauce, lemon juice, cumin, tahini, olive oil and water and puree until smooth, adding more water if necessary. Season with salt and pepper. Serve with Pepper Jack Crackers.

Celery Root Bisque Salad

I met Thomas Keller a long time ago at an event. He was serving a Jerusalem artichoke soup. This soup was so memorable that I tried to re-create it 20 years later. Of course I injected it with some Cajun flare by using smoky ham stock and with celery root. So here goes . . .

Serves 4

Pickled Radishes

1 lb (454 g) watermelon radishes, peeled quartered, then sliced

2 cups (475 ml) champagne vinegar

1 cup (237 ml) water

1 cup (200 g) sugar

1½ tsp (9 g) salt

Celery Root Bisque

½ cup (115 g) unsalted butter

1½ tbsp (13 g) minced garlic

4 cups (356 g) leeks, rinsed and diced

2½ lbs (1.1 kg) celery root, peeled and large diced

6 cups (1.4 L) Smoky Ham Stock (page 178)

2 bay leaves

1½ tsp (1 g) fresh thyme, chopped

4 cups (1 L) heavy cream

½ cup (118 ml) crème fraîche

Salt and white pepper, to taste

Black Pepper Scallops

8 small (20/30) sea scallops

2 tsp (9 g) unsalted butter

2 tsp (10 ml) extra-virgin olive oil

½ tsp salt

½ tsp black pepper, finely ground

½ tsp granulated garlic

Chive Oil (see page 172), to taste

For the pickled radishes, place the sliced radishes in a bowl. Put the vinegar, water, sugar and salt in a small saucepan and bring the mixture to a boil over high heat, stirring occasionally. Pour the liquid over the radishes, making sure the liquid covers them completely. Cool for 10 to 15 minutes, and then cover and refrigerate at least overnight before eating.

For the bisque, melt the butter in a heavy-bottomed saucepan over medium heat. Add the garlic and leeks and sweat for 5 minutes until softened (do not allow them to color). Add the celery root, Smoky Ham Stock, bay leaves and thyme and simmer until the vegetables are soft, 6 to 8 minutes. Add the heavy cream and return just to a boil. Remove from the heat. Remove the bay leaves and puree until smooth. Strain through a fine sieve and add the crème fraîche. Season with salt and white pepper.

For the scallops, remove the small side muscle from the scallops, rinse with cold water and thoroughly pat dry. Add the butter and olive oil to a medium-size sauté pan on high heat. Season the scallops with the salt, black pepper and granulated garlic. Once the fat begins to smoke, gently add the scallops, making sure they are not touching each other. Sear the scallops for 1 minute on each side. The scallops should have a ¼-inch (6-mm) golden crust on each side while still being translucent in the center.

To plate, ladle the bisque into a bowl and scatter the scallops around evenly. Top with 3 to 5 pickled radish slices, then drizzle with Chive Oil.

Cajun Guacamole with Blackened Shrimp

Although this guacamole might not be authentic in origin, it is authentic in flavor because Latin food actually uses a lot of the same ingredients like jalapeño, scallion, green tomato, etc. Lo and behold, this guacamole has become one of our best sellers. Who'd've thunk?

 SERVES 4

Guacamole

5 avocados, mashed

¼ cup (40 g) diced onion

2 tbsp (12 g) minced scallions

1 jalapeño, minced

2 tbsp (30 ml) lime juice

¼ cup (4 g) chopped cilantro

1 green tomato, small diced

1 tbsp (17 g) flaky sea salt

¼ tsp vitamin C powder or ascorbic acid (helps it stay green)

Salt and pepper, to taste

Blackened Shrimp

¾ lb (340 g) small shrimp, peeled and deveined, tails removed

Juice of 1 lemon

1½ tbsp (10 g) House Cajun Spice (page 155)

1 tbsp (15 ml) extra-virgin olive oil

Salt and pepper, to taste

BBQ Tortilla Chips

Canola oil, for frying

10 (6-inch [15-cm]) corn tortillas

1 tbsp (17 g) salt

2 tbsp (14 g) AKA Rub (page 154)

Garnishes

¼ cup (40 g) minced onion

¼ cup (24 g) grated cotija cheese

½ cup (8 g) micro cilantro or cilantro leaves

For the guacamole, combine the avocados, onion, scallions, jalapeño, lime juice, cilantro, green tomato, sea salt and vitamin C powder and mix until incorporated. Season with salt and pepper and cover with plastic wrap flush against the mixture to keep it from oxidizing and turning brown. Chill until ready to serve.

For the blackened shrimp, toss the shrimp with lemon juice and let it sit for 10 minutes. Drain the shrimp and pat dry. Sprinkle with the House Cajun Spice and toss to coat the shrimp. Let sit another 10 minutes or so. In a hot skillet over high heat, add the olive oil and then sauté the shrimp until just cooked, about 3 minutes. Season with salt and pepper, remove from the heat and chill.

For the chips, pour the canola oil into a pot fitted with a candy thermometer; you want the oil to be at least 1 inch (2.5 cm) deep. Heat the oil to about 360°F (182°C). Cut the tortillas in quarters and add them in batches to the hot oil without crowding them. Cook for 2 to 3 minutes, turning once to brown evenly. Remove the tortillas from the oil and drain them on paper towels. Continue cooking the chips in batches until they're all fried. Season liberally with salt and AKA Rub.

To plate, place the guacamole in a bowl and top with the blackened shrimp, minced onion, cotija cheese and micro cilantro leaves. Serve with chips on the side.

QUAHOG AND BACON CHOWDER

I am from Boston so I had to give a you a chowdah recipe—with a Lousiana spin, of course! People say all the time that this is bettah than Legal's kehd, those oystah crackers are wicked pissah. But allow me to translate: We do believe that your chowder is tastier than Legal Sea Foods' and we enjoy those lovely crackers on top. Bacon, cayenne and herbsaint scream New Orleans, kind of like a Bostonian screams at traffic.

◆ SERVES ABOUT 8 TO 10 ◆

Oyster Crackers

1 tbsp (7 g) Old Bay seasoning

2 tbsp (28 g) unsalted butter, melted

2 cups (90 g) oyster crackers

Chowder

½ cup (115 g) unsalted butter

1 cup (225 g) minced raw bacon

¾ cup (76 g) diced celery

¾ cup (115 g) diced onion

¾ cup (96 g) diced carrot

¾ cup (65 g) diced fennel

½ tsp cayenne

1 tsp fresh thyme leaves

1 bay leaf

½ cup (60 g) all-purpose flour

½ cup (118 ml) herbsaint

5 cups (1.2 L) clam juice

4 cups (908 g) quahog meat, large diced

1 lb (454 g) Yukon Gold potatoes, peeled and diced, cooked separate until just soft

¼ cup (15 g) finely chopped parsley

¼ cup (12 g) finely chopped fresh chives

Salt and pepper, to taste

Heavy cream, as needed

Garnishes

½ cup (56 g) crispy bacon bits

¼ cup (6 g) fresh tarragon, minced

To make the oyster crackers, preheat the oven to 350°F (177°C). Mix the Old Bay and melted butter in a small dish. Place the crackers in a medium-size bowl, pour the mixture over the crackers and toss until all the crackers are coated. Bake for 5 to 8 minutes. Remove from the oven and allow to cool.

To make the chowder, melt the butter in a large heavy pot over medium heat. Add the bacon and cook until the bacon begins to brown, about 8 minutes. Add the celery, onion, carrot, fennel, cayenne, thyme and bay leaf and sauté until the vegetables soften, about 6 minutes. Stir in the flour and cook for 2 minutes (do not allow the flour to brown). Gradually whisk in the herbsaint and clam juice. Add the quahog meat and potatoes and simmer the chowder for 10 to 15 minutes to blend the flavors, stirring frequently. Finish with the fresh parsley and chives and season with salt and pepper. Cool the chowder base until ready to use.

When ready to serve, heat the chowder base with heavy cream until the desired consistency is reached, and reseason if necessary. Garnish with oyster crackers, bacon bits and tarragon.

CRISPY, CRUNCHY DISHES

You know, if Grammy-winner Meghan Trainor just changed the word "bass" to "crunch," that would be the theme song to this chapter. Because you know I'm all about that crunch, 'bout that crunch.

This is the music of mastication. This is the auditory soundtrack to the sensory stimulus of eating. Science says that when you hear yourself crunch you tend to eat more. So what is the sonic appeal? I believe that sound affects your experience with food. I know "crunchy" will draw your attention because when I use the word "crunchy" or "crisp" on a menu, the item always sells better. These recipes have nothing in common; some are sides like the Celery Root Slaw (page 66) and some are small composed plates like the Buffalo Duck Wings (page 59), but they are all about those pleasant

Buffalo Duck Wings

Please don't let this recipe scare you because of the duck. Duck wings may not be the easiest to find, but I assure you it's well worth the scavenger hunt. If you can't find them, chicken wings will do the trick and are still so amazingly good. The coolest part of this recipe is that once you cook the wings in this style, you are now an expert at confiting, a very fancy cooking term! The confiting process, counterintuitively, helps render the fat more, which will then make these wings extra crunchy.

◆ **Serves 2 to 4** ◆

Buffalo Wings

1 dozen duck wings, split, wing tip removed

8 cups (2 L) canola oil, plus more for frying

2 cups (475 ml) Buttermilk Marinade (page 163)

Salt and pepper, to taste

¼ cup (59 ml) Buffalo Sauce (page 161), warmed

Blue Cheese–Celery Salad

1 tbsp (8 g) crumbled blue cheese

1 stalk celery, shaved with a potato peeler

1 radish, shaved thin

2 tsp (2 g) minced chives

1 tbsp (15 ml) Neutral Vinaigrette (page 172)

Salt and pepper, to taste

Plating

1 cup (237 ml) Buttermilk Ranch (page 177)

Preheat the oven to 300°F (149°C). Place the wings in a deep pan and cover with the canola oil. Place in the oven until the meat begins to pull away from bone, about 2 hours.

For the blue cheese–celery salad, mix together the blue cheese, celery, radish, chives and Neutral Vinaigrette. Season with salt and pepper

Once the wings are finished cooking, remove the wings from the oil and let them cool. Note: Reserve the oil for next time. The more you use it the better and more flavored it becomes. Once the wings are cool, soak the wings in the Buttermilk Marinade.

Preheat a deep fryer or a pot of oil to 360°F (182°C). Remove the wings from the marinade (discarding the marinade), and fry the wings until golden brown and crispy, 3 to 4 minutes. Season with salt and pepper and toss with warm Buffalo Sauce. Place the blue cheese–celery salad on top of the wings and either drizzle with Buttermilk Ranch or serve it on the side as a dipping sauce.

Andy's New-Style Fried Cod

I worked for Chef Andy Husbands for almost 7 years back in the day. I learned a ton and really got an opportunity to be around so many ingredients because we changed the menu often and did a lot of specials every night. This has helped me become the chef that I am today. The one thing you have to know about Andy is that he loves big, bold flavors and always adds an innovative twist like using rice flour instead of regular flour. This small change makes this dish crunchier than any other fried cod you have ever had.

Serves 6

Tartar Sauce

1¼ cups (296 ml) mayonnaise

1 medium-size kosher dill pickle, minced, plus 2 tbsp (30 ml) pickle juice

1 small red onion, peeled and minced

1 clove garlic, minced

1 tbsp (13 g) granulated sugar

1 tsp Old Bay seasoning

1 tbsp (15 ml) soy sauce

¼ cup (4 g) chopped cilantro leaves

Salt and pepper, to taste

Cod

2 lbs (907 g) cod filet, cut into ½-inch (12-mm) strips

Zest of 2 lemons

2–3 tsp (5–7 g) Old Bay seasoning

7 cups (1.1 kg) rice flour (non-gluten), divided

1 tsp cayenne pepper

2 tsp (9 g) baking powder

1 tbsp (17 g) salt

2 tsp (10 ml) sesame oil

6–7 cups (1.4–1.7 L) soda water

Canola oil, for frying

Salt and pepper, to taste

For the tartar sauce, combine the mayonnaise, dill pickle, onion, garlic, sugar, Old Bay, soy sauce, cilantro, salt and pepper in a small bowl, stir to mix thoroughly and set aside.

For the cod, place the fish on a sheet tray and evenly season on all sides with lemon zest and Old Bay. Let it sit, refrigerated, for 30 minutes to 3 hours. In a medium-size bowl, combine the cod and 2 cups (316 g) of the rice flour, tossing to coat. In a large bowl, combine the remaining 5 cups (790 g) of rice flour, cayenne, baking powder and salt. Add the sesame oil and 6 cups (1.4 L) of soda water; mix well. It should be a little thicker than pancake batter; add extra soda water as needed to achieve the right consistency.

Add the oil to a stockpot or Dutch oven to a depth of 4 inches (10 cm) and heat to 350°F (177°C). Test by dropping a piece of fish into the oil; it should sizzle vigorously and immediately on the surface without sinking or burning. When the oil is hot, lift a single cod piece out of the flour, lightly shaking off the excess, and drop it into the batter. Use tongs to transfer the coated pieces, one at a time, into the oil, frying in batches so as not to crowd the pan. As the fish fries, use the tongs to separate and move the pieces around. Fry until dark golden brown underneath, about 2 minutes; turn and cook the second side, 1 to 2 minutes more.

GARNISHES

1 bunch scallions, minced

1 cup (24 g) fresh basil leaves, roughly chopped

1 cup (24 g) fresh mint leaves, roughly chopped

Soy sauce, for seasoning

Sriracha or your favorite Asian hot sauce

½ cup (72 g) toasted sesame seeds

Remove the fish, allowing excess oil to drip back into the pan, then transfer to a plate lined with paper towels. Season with salt and pepper, then place on a serving platter.

Garnish with the scallions, basil and mint, lightly splash with soy sauce and drizzle with sriracha, then sprinkle with sesame seeds. Serve immediately with tartar sauce on the side.

Bourbon Barrel Ale–Battered Soft-shell Crabs

Although I do love soft-shell crab prepared any way, there is absolutely nothing more satisfying than taking a bite of a crunchy, fried soft-shell crab with some spicy mayonnaise and maybe a squeeze of fresh lemon on it. Add some green peas and this says summer all over it!

◆ **Serves 4** ◆

Crushed Peas

3 cups (435 g) English peas, shelled (from about 2 lbs [907 g] pods)

2 cloves garlic, minced

2 tsp (10 ml) lemon juice

¼ cup (59 ml) extra-virgin olive oil

2 tbsp (1 g) fresh dill

6 mint leaves

Salt and pepper, to taste

Tabasco Mayo

2 tbsp (8 g) finely chopped parsley leaves

2 tbsp (1 g) finely chopped fresh dill

1 clove garlic, minced

1 tsp lemon juice

1 tsp Dijon or Creole mustard

2 tsp (10 ml) or more Tabasco sauce

1 cup (237 ml) mayonnaise

2 tbsp (30 ml) sour cream

Salt and pepper, to taste

Battered Soft-Shell Crabs

1 cup (158 g) rice flour

⅓ cup (40 g) all-purpose flour

¼ tsp baking powder

¼ tsp cayenne

¼ tsp granulated garlic

1 tsp salt

1 (12-oz [355-ml]) bottle or can bourbon barrel ale

Canola oil, for frying

4 large soft-shell crabs, dressed

Salt and pepper, to taste

Fresh lemon

To make the crushed peas, bring a pot of salted water to a boil. Fill a bowl with ice water. Add the peas to the boiling water and cook until they begin to float, about 2 minutes. Do not overcook. Remove the peas fom the hot water and immediately plunge into the prepared ice bath. Once the peas are cool, drain and combine with the garlic, lemon juice, extra-virgin olive oil, dill and mint in a food processor, and pulse just until the pea mixture comes together but is still a bit chunky. Season with salt and pepper to taste and chill until ready to serve.

To make the Tabasco mayo, combine the parsley, dill, garlic, lemon juice, mustard, Tabasco, mayonnaise and sour cream in a bowl and mix. Season with salt and pepper to taste and chill until ready to serve.

To make the bourbon ale batter, whisk together the rice flour, all-purpose flour, baking powder, cayenne, granulated garlic, salt and beer. This is a light batter and should be on the thinner side.

In either a medium-size pot or a cast-iron pan, heat canola oil to 350°F (177°C). Dip each crab in the beer batter and fry until golden brown, about 3 minutes. Transfer to paper towels and drain. Season with salt and pepper. Serve atop peas with a side of Tabasco mayo and a wedge of fresh lemon.

Pepper Jack Crackers

I don't bake a lot, but when I do I bake crackers! Normally crackers are just a vehicle for a fantastic dip or spread, but this one is an exception. This is an extremely flavorful salty, crunchy, spicy cracker that you can just eat by itself as a snack (and trust me I do) or obviously jam into your favorite dip or spread such as the Boiled Peanut Hummus (page 49) or Buttermilk Onion Dip (page 69). Stored in an airtight container, these crackers will last awhile and can be used when needed. This recipe might seem random, but you need it in your life.

◆ **Makes about 20 large crackers** ◆

4 tbsp (57 g) cold unsalted butter, minced

½ cup (103 g) cold bacon fat

1 cup (80 g) grated Romano cheese

1 cup (113 g) grated pepper jack cheese

½ cup (118 ml) Natural Chicken Stock (page 179)

1 tbsp (15 ml) balsamic vinegar

2½ cups (312 g) all-purpose flour

1½ tsp (9 g) salt

½ tsp baking powder

1 tsp cayenne

1 tsp black pepper

2 tbsp (30 ml) honey

Flour, for rolling

Mix the butter with the bacon fat and keep cold. In a food processor, blend the cheeses until very fine. In a large mixing bowl, combine the butter and bacon fat mixture and the cheeses with the Natural Chicken Stock, vinegar, flour, salt, baking powder, cayenne, black pepper and honey and knead until the dough forms. Wrap the dough in plastic wrap and let chill in the refrigerator for at least 1 hour.

When ready to bake, preheat the oven to 350°F (177°C). Portion the dough into 2-tablespoon (28-g) balls. Line a baking sheet with a silicone baking mat or parchment paper.

On a floured work surface, roll out each dough ball very thin, about $1/16$ inch (1.5 mm). Transfer the dough to the prepared baking sheet and bake until golden brown, 15 to 17 minutes. Allow to cool before removing from the baking sheet into a container.

Celery Root Slaw

I thought you should have this really crunchy and refreshing recipe in your repertoire. I love the tastiness of this recipe. This can be served as a side, as a refreshing garnish on some wings or some fried chicken or as a bedding to something grilled. Or just put it on your burgers for an amazing contrast of crunch!

◆ **Serves 4 to 6 as a small side or much more for a crunchy garnish** ◆

2 small celery roots (about 1¼ lb [567 g] total), peeled and julienned into thin matchstick pieces or shredded

¼ cup (59 ml) mayonnaise

2 tbsp (30 ml) crème fraîche or sour cream

1 tbsp (9 g) dill pickle, minced

1 tbsp (4 g) fresh parsley leaves, minced

2 tsp (10 ml) lemon juice

½ tsp capers, drained and minced

½ tsp Dijon mustard

Pinch of dried tarragon, crumbled

Salt and pepper, to taste

Combine the celery roots, mayonnaise, crème fraîche, pickle, parsley, lemon juice, capers, mustard, tarragon, salt and pepper and chill. Ideally this should be served right away. It will hold a day or so in the fridge but will start to lose its crunch.

NOTE: I prefer Duke's brand mayonnaise. It might be harder to find in the North, so other mayonnaise brands will work too.

Sharp Cheddar Kettle Chips and Buttermilk Onion Dip

As simple as this sounds, cheddar and buttermilk are quintessential flavors of the South and go perfectly together. There is no denying that there is something religious about the crunch of a potato chip combined with an ice-cold dip. This is my go-to for a party or event when I don't have a lot of time but still need to show off a bit. I like to call this "the sleeper" because it comes across as simple, but it is always the most memorably delicious thing people ask me about. Plus, this is my mom's favorite, and she approves this message!

◆ ❰ Serves 4 as a snack ❱ ◆

Sharp Cheddar Spice

½ cup (60 g) cheddar cheese powder (taken from an instant mac & cheese box)

2 tsp (2 g) powdered thyme

2 tbsp (19 g) garlic salt

2 tbsp (14 g) onion powder

Potato Chips

2 large russet potatoes, scrubbed clean

8 cups (2 L) canola oil, for frying

Salt and pepper, to taste

Buttermilk Onion Dip

2 tbsp (30 ml) extra-virgin olive oil

1 lb (454 g) Spanish onions, minced

¼ tsp granulated garlic

1 tsp celery salt

2 tsp (2 g) dried thyme leaves

1 tbsp (15 g) granulated sugar

3 tbsp (44 ml) Worcestershire sauce

¼ tsp ground white pepper

½ tsp salt

1½ cups (355 ml) sour cream

¾ cup (177 ml) mayonnaise

To make the sharp cheddar spice, mix the cheddar cheese powder, thyme, garlic salt and onion powder and store in an airtight container until ready to use.

To make the potato chips, start by using a mandoline or a very sharp knife to slice the potatoes into thin rounds. Place the potatoes in a large bowl of water to prevent discoloration. Heat the oil in a large, heavy pot or kettle to approximately 340°F (171°C). Pat the potatoes completely dry and fry in batches, cooking until golden brown, about 2 minutes. Drain on paper towels and while still warm, season with salt, pepper and the cheddar spice.

To make the buttermilk onion dip, place a sauté pan over medium heat. Add the oil and the onions and cook, stirring, for about 15 minutes, until deeply caramelized. Remove from the heat and set aside to cool. Combine the garlic, celery salt, thyme, sugar, Worcestershire sauce, pepper, salt, sour cream and mayonnaise with the cooled onions. Refrigerate until needed and stir before serving.

Cast Iron–Baked Brie

I know what you're thinking: Why is soft Brie in the Crispy, Crunchy Dishes chapter? I'll tell you why! It's because the fresh gooseberries give you a nice snap, the almonds are super crunchy, the tasso ham bits are crispy and the focaccia, which in my opinion makes this dish, is so crunchy when grilled. The Brie is like butter and just melts into the bread and you're left with an amazingly crunchy bite.

Serves 4 to 8 as an appetizer

Cane Syrup

¼ cup (59 ml) Madeira wine

¼ cup (59 ml) apple cider vinegar

¼ cup (59 ml) cane syrup (I prefer Steen's brand) or molasses

¼ cup (50 g) sugar

1 small sprig rosemary

2 sprigs thyme

1 bay leaf

Salt and pepper, to taste

Baked Brie

1 (8-oz [227-g]) Brie wheel

2 cups (300 g) gooseberries, husks removed and halved

½ cup (72 g) smoked almonds, rough chopped

½ cup (68 g) tasso ham, minced and sautéed until crispy

1 cup (60 g) mixed herb leaves (parsley, tarragon, chervil)

1-inch (2.5-cm) thick slab focaccia, grilled

For the cane syrup, combine the Madeira, vinegar, cane syrup, sugar, rosemary, thyme and bay leaf in a small pot and bring all the ingredients to a boil. Remove the mixture from the heat and strain, then season to taste with salt and pepper. Reserve 1 cup (237 ml) for the Brie and save the rest for another time. The syrup can be refrigerated in an airtight container for up to a month.

Preheat the oven to 350°F (177°C) and place the Brie in a cast-iron pan slightly larger than the cheese. Top with the cane syrup and bake for 10 to 12 minutes or until the Brie is still whole but feels very soft. Top with the gooseberries, smoked almonds and crispy tasso bits. Garnish with the mixed herbs and serve with grilled focaccia.

FISH WITH SHELLS

As the great Benjamin Buford Blue, aka Bubba, once said: "Anyway, like I was sayin', shrimp is the fruit of the sea. You can barbecue it, boil it, broil it, bake it, sauté it. Dey's uh, shrimp-kabobs, shrimp Creole, shrimp gumbo. Pan fried, deep fried, stir-fried. There's pineapple shrimp, lemon shrimp, coconut shrimp, pepper shrimp, shrimp soup, shrimp stew, shrimp salad, shrimp and potatoes, shrimp burger, shrimp sandwich. That—that's about it." WAIT! There is more I say! Don't forget about crawfish and mussels and oysters. This chapter is all about the vast variety of exceptionally fresh and abundant shellfish out there. Keep it fresh, y'all!

Crawfish and Crab Soup

This is almost like a gumbo, minus the okra and not as thick, but the flavor is definitely there. I think soup can sometimes be overlooked, but this recipe delivers on satisfaction.

◆ **Serves 4 to 5** ◆

½ cup (115 g) unsalted butter, divided

½ cup (60 g) all-purpose flour

2 cups (300 g) diced onion

2 cups (202 g) diced celery

2 cups (300 g) diced green bell pepper

1 tbsp (8 g) minced garlic

1 tbsp (7 g) House Cajun Spice (page 155)

1 tbsp (6 g) filé gumbo powder

⅓ cup (78 ml) absinthe

1 (28-oz [794-g]) can diced tomatoes, including juice

1 cup (154 g) corn kernels

8 cups (2 L) Lobster Stock (page 181)

2 bay leaves

1 cup (135 g) crab meat

2 cups (290 g) crawfish tail meat

½ cup (30 g) finely chopped parsley

1 bunch scallions, finely chopped

Salt and pepper, to taste

Preheat the oven to 350°F (177°C).

To make a roux, bake 4 tablespoons (57 g) of butter and the flour for 45 minutes in a small casserole dish, whisking every 15 minutes throughout the cooking process. Don't burn it!

In a heavy-bottomed pot over medium heat, add the remaining 4 tablespoons (57 g) of butter and sauté the onion, celery, green pepper and garlic until slightly caramelized, about 5 minutes. Add in the roux, House Cajun Spice and filé and cook for 2 minutes. Deglaze with the absinthe, then add the tomatoes, corn, Lobster Stock and bay leaves, and bring to a boil. Simmer for 30 minutes. Add the crab meat and crawfish and cook for 2 more minutes; you don't want to overcook the shellfish. Remove from the heat and add the parsley and scallions. Season with salt and pepper.

Lemon Shandy-Poached Peel-and-Eat Shrimp

I think everybody and their sister has some version of shrimp cocktail. I tried to come up with a cool way to inject that Southern smack and do justice to such an iconic dish while not serving the otherwise obligatory bland, rubbery shrimp and crappy store-bought cocktail sauce circa the '80s. The only cardinal rules are don't overcook the shrimp and don't be lazy and buy already peeled shrimp, because you are losing flavor and my personal trust by not cooking them in their shells.

◆━━ **Serves 4 as an appetizer** ━━◆

2 tbsp (30 ml) liquid crab boil

2 tbsp (14 g) crab boil powder (I like Zatarain's, but Old Bay works as well)

2 lemons, halved, plus more for serving

2 bay leaves

1 bunch parsley

1 (12-oz [355-ml]) bottle or can lemon shandy beer

4 cups (1 L) water

1 lb (454 g) U-12 shrimp with the shell on (see Note)

Crystal Cocktail Sauce (page 80), for serving

In a large pot, add the liquid crab boil, crab boil powder, halved lemons, bay leaves, parsley, beer and water. Bring the mixture to a boil, then reduce the heat and simmer for about 5 minutes to infuse all that flavor. Add the shrimp and cook uncovered for exactly 5 minutes, until the shrimp are bright pink.

Remove the pot from the heat and add 1 gallon (3.75 L) of ice to the pot immediately in order to stop the cooking process. Four cubes are not enough; it may seem like overkill, but it has to be enough to truly chill it almost immediately. That way the shrimp can chill in flavorful liquid versus taking them out and putting them in ice water. Once cold, remove the shrimp from the liquid and get peeling! Serve the peeled shrimp with fresh lemon and Crystal Cocktail Sauce.

NOTE: Shrimp come in all sizes and U-12 means you will get under 12 per pound (450 g), so pretty big. That means if you buy 21/25s you will get 21-25 per pound (450 g). Get it? The lower the number the higher your ego gets when you are making this for guests!

Louisiana-Style Mussels

I love mussels, but I love the mixture they are cooked in even more. Something about the juice that comes out of those bad boys brings your sauce game from great to perfection!

1 clove garlic, minced

¼ cup (34 g) diced tasso ham

1 tbsp (10 g) minced shallots

¼ red bell pepper, medium diced

1 tbsp (15 ml) extra-virgin olive oil

2 lbs (907 g) mussels, scrubbed clean

1 tsp fresh thyme, chopped

½ cup (118 ml) Lobster Stock (page 181) (or any seafood stock)

1 tbsp (15 ml) lemon juice

1 tsp House Cajun Spice (page 155)

1 tsp lemon pepper

1 tsp Creole spice (I prefer Zatarain's)

1 tsp hot sauce

¼ cup (66 g) black-eyed peas, cooked or canned

Crusty bread, for serving

Sauté the garlic, tasso ham, shallots and bell pepper in extra-virgin olive oil until soft, about 5 minutes, then add the mussels and cook for 1 minute. Add the thyme, Lobster Stock, lemon juice, Cajun spice, lemon pepper, Creole spice and hot sauce and cook until the mussels are open and cooked, about 5 minutes. Finish with the black-eyed peas and serve in a bowl with crusty bread.

Oysters On The Half Shell With 3 Sauces

Not sure who would have thought to pull an oyster out of the ocean, break open the shell and consume it. Sounds kind of crazy, right? But thank God that happened, because oysters are one of my favorite things ever. I could eat my weight in them any day, any time. The sauces I like to serve with them are great and go perfectly in my opinion. I am the guy who never likes to eat an oyster the same way twice—so here you have my three favorite ways to serve them.

◆ MAKES 2 CUPS (475 ML) SAUCE ◆

Atomic Horseradish Cream

¼ cup (60 g) prepared horseradish
2 tbsp (30 ml) sherry vinegar
2¼ tsp (5 g) mustard powder
½ cup (118 ml) mayonnaise
1 cup (237 ml) sour cream
¼ tsp red pepper flakes

Pink Pepper Mignonette

1 cup (237 ml) rosé champagne
1 cup (237 ml) raspberry champagne vinegar
1 shallot, minced
2 tsp (5 g) pink peppercorns, crushed
Pinch of salt

Crystal Cocktail Sauce

1 cup (237 ml) ketchup
1½ tsp (7 ml) Worcestershire sauce
¼ cup (59 ml) lemon juice
1½ tsp (8 g) prepared horseradish
½ cup (118 g) hot sauce (I prefer Crystal brand)
1 tbsp (15 ml) molasses
¾ tsp onion powder
¾ tsp oregano
¼ tsp ground cloves
¼ tsp salt
¼ tsp coarse black pepper

For the Atomic Horseradish Cream

Whisk together the horseradish, vinegar, mustard powder, mayonnaise, sour cream and red pepper flakes.

For the Pink Pepper Mignonette

Mix together the champagne, vinegar, shallot, crushed peppercorns and salt.

For the Crystal Cocktail Sauce

Whisk together the ketchup, Worcestershire sauce, lemon juice, horseradish, hot sauce, molasses, onion powder, oregano, cloves, salt and pepper.

Roasted Chargrilled Oysters

This recipe is inspired by Felix's, the first restaurant I visited on my very first trip to New Orleans. This place is famous for its chargrilled oysters. A guy there literally stands in a Plexiglas® box grilling oysters all day. Why the box, you ask? Because all the butter melting into the grill creates a 5-alarm fire's worth of smoke. I do not own any Plexiglas, and I am guessing you don't either, so I took the flavors from those oysters, incorporated them into the butter and just roasted them instead of you having to deal with smoke equivalent to a space shuttle reentering the atmosphere. Oh, and by the way, my wife and I ate 8 dozen of those oysters in 48 hours. Both disturbing and amazing all at the same time, no?

◆ **Makes 2 dozen oysters** ◆

Chargrilled Butter

1 cup (227 g) unsalted butter, softened

2 tbsp (30 ml) extra-virgin olive oil

1½ tsp (7 ml) Worcestershire sauce

1½ tsp (7 ml) lemon juice

1½ tsp (7 ml) white wine

1½ tsp (4 g) ground white pepper

1½ tsp (3 g) black pepper

1½ tsp (5 g) granulated onion

1½ tsp (5 g) granulated garlic

1½ tsp (2 g) Italian seasoning

¼ tsp liquid smoke

½ tsp salt

Lemon Breadcrumbs

1½ cups (135 g) panko breadcrumbs

½ cup (40 g) grated Romano cheese

¼ cup (57 g) unsalted butter, melted

2 tbsp (17 g) lemon pepper

1 tbsp (4 g) minced fresh parsley

Zest and juice of 1 lemon

Oysters

24 of your favorite oysters, shucked and in the half shell

Lemon wedges, for serving

For the chargrilled butter, place the butter, olive oil, Worcestershire sauce, lemon juice, white wine, white pepper, black pepper, onion, garlic, Italian seasoning, liquid smoke and salt in a stand mixer with the whip attachment. Whip until light and airy. Essentially this is a compound butter. Besides the oysters, you can smear this butter on steak, toss some wings in it or use it anywhere in place of regular butter for an additional blast of flavor.

For the lemon breadcrumbs, mix the breadcrumbs, Romano cheese, melted butter, lemon pepper, parsley and lemon zest and juice until well combined.

To roast the oysters, preheat the oven to 450°F (232°C). Crinkle some aluminum foil on a baking sheet or sprinkle some salt on it to keep the oysters from tipping over. Place the oysters on the baking sheet, shell-side down. Evenly spoon the whipped butter on each oyster, then top with the breadcrumb mixture. Bake for 10 to 12 minutes or until the oysters are curled and the breadcrumbs are nicely browned. Serve with a fresh wedge of lemon.

Pan-Seared Sea Scallops And tasso ham

This is one of the first dishes I was allowed to put on the menu as a young chef. It has changed over the years, but it is undeniable that scallops and bacon are a classic combination. We use tasso ham, but you get the idea.

◆ ◄ Serves 4 as an appetizer ► ◆

Tabasco-Soaked Cherries

¼ cup (40 g) dried cherries

¼ cup (59 ml) boiling water

1 tbsp (15 ml) Tabasco sauce

Molasses Aioli

2 tbsp (30 ml) mayonnaise

2 tbsp (30 ml) molasses

1 clove garlic, minced

½ tsp red wine vinegar

1 tsp chives, minced

Salt and pepper, to taste

Almond Crumble

2 tbsp (12 g) smoked almonds, crushed

2 tbsp (16 g) all-purpose flour

¼ cup (24 g) almond flour

1 tsp salt

2 tbsp (28 g) unsalted butter, softened

Scallops & Tasso Ham

1 tbsp (15 ml) blended oil

⅛-inch (3-mm) thick slices tasso ham

8 sea scallops

Salt and pepper, to taste

Plating

2 tbsp (6 g) fresh minced chives

For the Tabasco cherries, mix the cherries, boiling water and Tabasco together and let soak for 30 minutes, then strain and discard the liquid.

For the molasses aioli, whisk together the mayonnaise, molasses, garlic, vinegar and chives and season with salt and pepper to taste.

For the almond crumble, preheat the oven to 300°F (149°C). In a small bowl, combine the almonds, all-purpose flour, almond flour, salt and butter and place the mixture on a cookie sheet. Bake for 8 to 10 minutes or until golden brown. Let cool to room temperature.

For the scallops, heat a large sauté pan over medium-high heat. Add the blended oil and tasso ham and cook until the ham has a nice crisp to it. Remove the ham and keep warm. Season the scallops with salt and pepper. In the same pan on medium-high heat, sear the scallops on both sides, approximately 1 minute on each side, to a perfect medium-rare. Place the tasso ham on a plate and top with the cherries.

Place the scallops on top, drizzle with molasses aioli and garnish with chives and almond crumble.

SUNDAY FUNDAY

I have been cooking brunch all my career, and it's honestly a love-hate relationship. I love cooking breakfast food, which is obviously huge not just in New Orleans but everywhere, but I just don't like getting up that early! After digging deep, though, I figured I would get up early for you and compile some of my most favorite and unique items that we serve. I purposely didn't put an omelet recipe in here. Know why? Because they are dumb! Cook fun and keep it easy like Sunday morning.

Biscuits and Gravy 2.0

The reason this is 2.0 is because everybody has had the old-school white sausage gravy over biscuits in their life and yes, this is kinda the same but with better gravy, better biscuits and house made andouille sausage . . . plus 3.0 was taken. I like to put the sausage on top versus in the gravy because I think it looks better and I like to be able to taste each component separately and give some added texture.

Serves 0

1 tbsp (14 g) unsalted butter

1 cup (150 g) minced onion

½ cup (60 g) all-purpose flour

½ tsp paprika

½ tsp garlic powder

¼ tsp cayenne

4 cups (1 L) half & half

¼ cup (59 ml) meat juice (demi-glace, beef broth, pork stock, meat drippings, etc.)

Salt and pepper, to taste

3 cups (750 g) ground Andouille Sausage (page 28)

8 warm Buttermilk & Bourbon's Honey-Glazed Biscuits (page 13), split

2 tbsp (6 g) minced chives, for garnish

In a medium-size saucepan, heat the butter over medium heat and sweat the onion just until soft with no color. Whisk in the flour, paprika, garlic powder and cayenne and cook, stirring, for 5 minutes. Add the half & half and meat juice and whisk until smooth. Reduce the heat and slowly simmer for 15 minutes until thick and bubbly. Season with salt and pepper.

In a separate small sauté pan over medium heat, cook the Andouille Sausage until it is fully cooked and crumbled.

To serve, place a biscuit on each plate, smother with the gravy and top with the crumbled Andouille Sausage. Garnish with the chives.

Deviled Egg Toast with Country ham and hot pepper salaD

Country ham and eggs are the influence on this, obviously. This was one of the first dishes I came up with when I was writing our first menu. I love deviled eggs—who doesn't? I wanted to come up with something original but still really yummy. The bread is important. We use bread from Iggy's in Cambridge, Massachusetts. They have, in my opinion, the best focaccia in the history of focaccia, but regardless, you want to use a very high-quality bread for this one. Don't be cheap! I'm watching you . . .

Serves 4

10 eggs (plus 2 extra in case you need a snack while making this)

1 tsp kosher salt

1 tsp white vinegar

2 tbsp (30 ml) mayonnaise

1 tbsp (15 ml) Dijon mustard

1 tbsp (15 ml) lemon juice

½ tsp hot sauce

½ tsp Worcestershire sauce

Pinch of cayenne

Salt and pepper, to taste

¼ cup (26 g) Hot Cherry Peppers (page 31)

½ cup (24 g) fresh mixed herb leaves/pieces (parsley, dill, chives, chervil)

2 radishes, shaved thin

1 tsp Neutral Vinaigrette (page 172)

4 slices grilled or toasted focaccia

4 tbsp (57 g) Chargrilled Butter (page 83)

4 slices very thinly sliced country ham or prosciutto

Place the eggs in a heavy pot, cover with an inch (2.5 cm) of water, then add the kosher salt and white vinegar, bring to a simmer and cook for 10 minutes. Meanwhile, prepare an ice bath by filling a bowl with ice water. After the eggs have finished cooking, remove them to the ice water to cool completely. Gently crack the eggs by rolling them along a counter. Peel the eggs carefully, then dice them and set aside.

Whisk together the mayonnaise, Dijon mustard, lemon juice, hot sauce, Worcestershire sauce and cayenne and season with salt and pepper to taste. Mix with the eggs and set aside. Mix together the Hot Cherry Peppers, herbs, radishes and vinaigrette.

To plate, place the warm focaccia on the plate and liberally smear it with the Chargrilled Butter. Top with the sliced ham and the egg mixture and garnish with the hot pepper salad. Serve immediately.

Crab Meat and Bacon Hash With poached duck eggs

Yes, I know we all secretly love that corned beef hash in a can, but that is something you eat in a dark room with an air conditioner on in solitude. This hash is off the charts in deliciousness and so full of flavor it's crazy! Do not let the duck egg thing scare you away. Obviously, you can use chicken eggs, but duck eggs in my opinion are a little bit richer, a little bit tastier, a little bit bigger and super cool (and honestly not that hard to come by).

 Serves 6

5 tbsp (71 g) unsalted butter, divided

¼ cup (28 g) crisped bacon bits

9 medium-size red bliss potatoes, ½ inch (12 mm) diced and blanched

1 cup (150 g) diced onion

1 cup (100 g) diced celery

1 cup (149 g) diced red bell pepper

1 cup (149 g) diced poblano pepper

1 cup (149 g) diced yellow bell pepper

1 tbsp (6 g) seeded and minced jalapeño

2 cloves garlic, minced

1 lb (454 g) jumbo lump crab meat, picked over for shells

2 tsp (5 g) paprika

Pinch of cayenne

3 tbsp (19 g) minced scallions

Salt and pepper, to taste

1 tbsp (15 ml) white vinegar

12 duck eggs

Hot Sauce Hollandaise (page 94), for serving

In a large nonstick pan, heat 3 tablespoons (43 g) of the butter over medium heat until hot. Add the bacon and potatoes and sauté until golden brown, about 8 to 10 minutes. In another nonstick pan, melt the remaining 2 tablespoons (28 g) of butter over medium heat. Add the onion, celery, peppers and garlic, and sauté until soft, about 3 to 5 minutes. Toss in the cooked potatoes, crab meat, paprika, cayenne and scallions. Season with salt and pepper and keep warm.

Bring a wide, shallow pan of water to a boil. Add the vinegar and a pinch of salt and lower the heat so the water is at a simmer, 160 to 180°F (71 to 82°C). Break the duck eggs into the pan and poach for 3 minutes. Lift each egg out with a slotted spoon and drain briefly on a paper towel. Serve the hash topped with poached eggs and Hot Sauce Hollandaise.

Hot Sauce Hollandaise

I could be wrong, but I feel like people are generally afraid to make hollandaise. They believe it's so labor-intensive. Honestly, it's easy and can be used on so many different things. Once you master it—and I promise you, you will—it's a great thing to know how to make. Some chefs say to use clarified butter, but I like to just use melted butter because the milk solids help thin it out and give the sauce a good creamy consistency. Oh yeah . . . and use a food processor to make this—you will thank me later.

◆ **Makes 1½ cups (355 ml)** ◆

1 cup (227 g) unsalted butter

1 sprig thyme

1 shallot, diced small

4 egg yolks

Juice of ½ lemon

1 tbsp (15 ml) or more of hot sauce

2 tsp (10 ml) Worcestershire sauce

Cayenne, to taste

Salt and pepper, to taste

Put the butter, thyme and diced shallot in a small saucepan and cook slowly in order to infuse the butter and cook the shallot. When the butter is melted, remove the thyme sprig and discard.

In a food processor, combine the egg yolks, lemon juice, hot sauce and Worcestershire sauce. While the machine is running, drizzle in the warm butter mixture in a slow, steady stream until the mixture is emulsified and creamy. Season with the cayenne, salt and pepper. Serve immediately or gently keep warm until needed.

Red Velvet Pancakes

Red velvet, cream cheese and pecans are as Southern as it gets. Keep calm and eat your pancakes!

Cream Cheese Glaze

¼ cup (57 g) cream cheese, softened

¼ cup (59 ml) heavy cream

1 tbsp (13 g) sugar

1 tsp vanilla paste

1 tsp orange zest

Blueberry-Pecan Syrup

½ cup (115 g) unsalted butter

½ cup (55 g) pecan pieces

½ cup (59 ml) cane syrup (I prefer Steen's brand)

2 tsp (9 g) vanilla paste

1 cup (148 g) blueberries

1 tbsp (15 ml) water

Pinch of salt

Pancakes

2 cups (240 g) all-purpose flour

2 tbsp (11 g) cocoa powder

1 tsp baking soda

1 tsp salt

2 tbsp (25 g) sugar

2 eggs, lightly beaten

2 tbsp (28 g) unsalted butter, melted

2 cups (475 ml) buttermilk

1 tbsp (12 g) vanilla paste

Few drops of red food coloring

Garnish

1 cup (148 g) blueberries

2 tbsp (16 g) powdered sugar

4 sprigs mint

For the cream cheese glaze, in a stand mixer fitted with the paddle attachment and on the lowest setting, combine the cream cheese, heavy cream, sugar, vanilla paste and orange zest until well incorporated. Increase the speed and whip the ingredients together until smooth, light and airy.

For the blueberry-pecan syrup, preheat a heavy-bottomed pot over medium heat. Add the butter and let it begin to melt. When the butter is mostly melted, add the pecan pieces. Cook for about 3 minutes, stirring constantly, until the pecans are well toasted and have a rich brown color. When the butter begins to foam around the pecan pieces, add the cane syrup all at once. Continue to cook the butter-syrup mixture until it is hot and bubbly, about 5 minutes. Momentarily remove the pan from the heat and carefully add the vanilla paste, blueberries and water, incorporating with a whisk or wooden spoon. Return the pan to the heat and cook the mixture for 3 to 4 more minutes, until the mixture is hot and thickens slightly. Add a pinch of salt. Remove from the heat and keep warm.

For the pancakes, preheat a lightly greased or nonstick skillet on the stovetop over medium-low heat. In a large bowl, whisk together the flour, cocoa powder, baking soda, salt and sugar. Add the eggs, melted butter, buttermilk, vanilla paste and red food coloring and whisk well until the batter is smooth and very few lumps remain. Drop the batter onto the hot skillet and cook until the edges just start to set and the bottom is lightly browned. Turn once and cook again until the bottom is lightly browned.

To plate, place a stack of pancakes in the center of the plate and spoon some of the blueberry-pecan syrup over the top. Place a dollop of cream cheese glaze on top of that, then garnish with fresh blueberries, powdered sugar and fresh mint sprigs.

*See photo on page 86.

NOTE: Vanilla paste is a cross between the bean and extract. You can equally substitute extract for the paste.

Crispy Soft-Boiled Eggs with Pastrami Home Fries

When people try this they wonder two things. One is: How on earth did you make that egg fried but still liquid in the middle? The second is: Where have these home fries been all my life?

Serves 4

Smoked Mayo

1 roasted red pepper, peeled

2 tbsp (30 ml) red wine vinegar

1½ tsp (7 ml) liquid smoke

2 cups (475 ml) mayonnaise

Smoked salt, to taste

Pastrami Home Fries

¼ cup (57 g) unsalted butter

1 lb (454 g) black pastrami, diced

2 lbs (907 g) red bliss potatoes, parcooked and sliced ¼ inch (6 mm) thick

1 cup (150 g) diced onion

1 cup (100 g) diced celery

1 cup (149 g) diced green bell pepper

1 tbsp (8 g) minced garlic

2 tbsp (14 g) black pepper, coarsely ground

1 tbsp (7 g) smoked paprika

1 tbsp (6 g) mustard powder

1½ tsp (3 g) coriander, ground

1½ tsp (4 g) white pepper, ground

1½ tsp (9 g) smoked salt

⅛ tsp cayenne

Crispy Soft-Boiled Eggs

10 eggs, room temperature

1½ cups (180 g) all-purpose flour

4 eggs, beaten

2 cups (180 g) panko breadcrumbs, ground fine

Oil, for frying

½ cup (24 g) minced chives, to garnish

For the smoked mayo, use a food processor to puree the roasted red pepper with the red wine vinegar and liquid smoke, then combine with the mayonnaise and season with smoked salt.

For the pastrami home fries, heat the butter in a large cast-iron pan until hot. Add the pastrami and potatoes and cook until golden brown and crispy, about 8 to 10 minutes. Stir in the onion, celery, green pepper, garlic, black pepper, paprika, mustard powder, coriander, white pepper, smoked salt and cayenne and cook for 10 more minutes.

For the eggs, bring a pot of water to a rolling boil, then drop 10 eggs in and cook them for precisely 5 minutes 30 seconds while you prepare an ice bath by adding ice cubes to a bowl of ice water. Immediately plunge the eggs into the ice bath. Next gently peel the eggs, as they will be very delicate. You will probably lose a couple to breakage, but that's okay—that's why you cooked 10. Roll the eggs in the flour, then the beaten egg, then the panko crumbs. Heat oil in a deep pan to 350°F (177°C) and fry the eggs until golden brown and crispy (be careful not to overcook; yolk should still be very runny).

To plate, place the crispy eggs on top of the home fries in the cast-iron pan. Drizzle with the smoked mayo and garnish with fresh minced chives.

Andouille Scotch Eggs

These will mess your world up, they're so monumentally good. It's your job to spread the word on these. I feel like Scotch eggs are not as mainstream as they should be, and people are missing out. If you live in New Orleans your middle name is probably andouille. Make scotch eggs great again!

◆ ⟨ MAKES 8 ⟩ ◆

Pickled Onions

½ lb (227 g) red onions, sliced thin

1 cup (237 ml) red wine vinegar

½ cup (100 g) sugar

½ cup (118 ml) water

2 tsp (12 g) salt

Andouille Scotch Eggs

10 large eggs, divided

1 lb (454 g) loose Andouille Sausage (page 28)

Canola oil, for frying

1 cup (120 g) all-purpose flour

2 cups (180 g) panko breadcrumbs, finely ground

Salt and pepper, to taste

Creole Mayo

1 cup (237 ml) mayonnaise

2 tbsp (30 ml) Creole mustard

2 tbsp (30 g) prepared horseradish

1 tsp Tabasco sauce

½ tsp sugar

1 clove garlic, minced

Salt and pepper, to taste

Watercress leaves, for serving

For the pickled red onions, place the sliced onions in a bowl. Bring the vinegar, sugar, water and salt to a boil over high heat, stirring occasionally. Pour the hot liquid over the onions, making sure the liquid covers them completely. Cool 10 to 15 minutes, and then cover and refrigerate overnight before eating.

For the Scotch eggs, bring a half gallon (1.9 L) of water to a boil in a medium-size saucepan. Meanwhile, fill a medium-size bowl half with ice and half with water. Using a slotted spoon, gently slide 8 eggs into the boiling water and cook for 6 minutes. Remove the eggs and immediately place in the ice bath. Gently peel the eggs, being careful not to break them. You might want to cook 1 or 2 extra just to be sure! Reserve the eggs in the ice bath. Divide the Andouille Sausage into 8 equal portions. One at a time, smash each sausage ball into a flat disk the diameter of your hand. Wrap each sausage disk carefully around an egg. Make sure that you completely encase the eggs in the sausage mixture. Once done, cover the eggs with plastic wrap and refrigerate until chilled, at least 1 hour or overnight if you want to get ahead.

Meanwhile, prepare the Creole mayo by whisking together the mayonnaise, mustard, horseradish, Tabasco, sugar and garlic. Season with salt and pepper.

When ready to cook the eggs, heat a pot with 2 inches (5 cm) of oil to 350°F (177°C). Line a plate with paper towels. Whisk the remaining 2 eggs in a small bowl. Place the flour and panko crumbs in separate small bowls. Carefully roll the eggs in the flour, then the egg mix and then the ground panko. Fry the eggs in the hot oil for about 4 minutes, just until the sausage is cooked but the egg yolk is still slightly runny—this does take some practice to perfectly cook. Once done, transfer the eggs to the paper towels and season with salt and pepper to taste.

To plate, gently cut each egg in half lengthwise with a serrated knife. Place some watercress on a plate and arrange both halves yolk-side up. Season the egg yolks with salt and pepper. Garnish with pickled red onions and a dollop of Creole mayo. Serve hot.

LEAVES & DRESSINGS

"Let's take a trip to New Orleans and get some salad," said no one ever! However, I feel like most people would say this if they tried my Baby Spinach Salad (page 110). So maybe you don't think of New Orleans and salad at the same time, but maybe you should start . . . with this chapter. Am I a trendsetter? I don't know. But the moral of the story is that these are all damn good and deserve real estate in this book. I salute you, Mr. Leafy Green Goodness.

Heirloom Tomato Salad

This is a great summer salad. I find that the addition of the fines herbes (always parsley, chives, chervil and tarragon) brings an amazing freshness and a stunning presentation along with all the different colors. Make sure you use a good feta cheese that is nice and creamy versus that generic crumbly stuff you find everywhere.

Serves 4

8 heirloom cherry tomatoes, halved

4 heirloom tomatoes, cut in narrow wedges

8 kalamata olives, pitted and halved

2 tbsp (18 g) pepperoncini, sliced

½ cup (75 g) julienned red onion

½ cup (60 g) sliced English cucumber

½ cup (75 g) feta cheese, diced

½ cup (59 ml) House Vinaigrette (page 106)

1 tbsp (4 g) fresh parsley leaves

1 tbsp (3 g) fresh minced chives

1 tbsp (4 g) fresh chervil leaves

1 tbsp (4 g) fresh tarragon leaves

Salt and pepper, to taste

Mix the tomatoes, olives, pepperoncini, red onion, cucumber and feta with the House Vinaigrette. Top with the fresh herbs and salt and pepper to taste.

Sweet Gem Salad

This was a salad we made when I was on *Hell's Kitchen* on FOX. Yes, it was a TV show. Yes, there was a ton of yelling—but we made such good food, honestly. This is my favorite salad by Gordon Ramsay.

SERVES 4

4 heads sweet gem lettuce

½ cup (118 ml) Truffle Vinaigrette (page 107)

Salt and pepper, to taste

16 red seedless grapes, halved

½ cup (59 g) Candied Walnuts (page 122)

½ cup (68 g) crumbled Clemson blue cheese or any type of Gorgonzola

Mix the lettuce and Truffle Vinaigrette together. Season with salt and pepper and top with the grapes, walnuts and cheese.

House Vinaigrette

This is one of my favorites because it has a nice flavorful, yet mellow taste that works well when you want the vinaigrette to take a back seat and let the other ingredients be the star.

◆ **Makes about 2 cups (475 ml)** ◆

1½ tsp (7 ml) Dijon mustard

6 tbsp (90 ml) red wine vinegar

6 tbsp (90 ml) water

1½ tsp (5 g) garlic powder

1½ tsp (2 g) dried oregano

1½ tsp (1 g) dried basil

1½ tsp (3 g) black pepper

1½ tsp (3 g) onion powder

1 tsp salt

½ cup (118 ml) extra-virgin olive oil

½ cup (118 ml) blended oil

In a blender, combine the mustard, vinegar, water, garlic powder, oregano, basil, black pepper, onion powder and salt. With the blender running, drizzle in the oils in a slow steady stream in order to emulsify. Store in the refrigerator for up to 2 weeks.

TRUFFLE VINAIGRETTE

This is an extremely flavorful vinaigrette that should be used sparingly. This will leave a lasting impression on a salad or would be great on some grilled vegetables.

¼ cup (59 ml) water

2 tsp (10 ml) Dijon mustard

¼ cup (59 ml) mayonnaise

2 tbsp (30 ml) lemon juice

¼ cup (48 g) canned black truffle peelings

¼ cup (59 ml) white truffle oil

¼ cup (59 ml) blended oil

1 tbsp (4 g) minced fresh parsley

Salt and pepper, to taste

In a blender, combine the water, mustard, mayonnaise, lemon juice and black truffle and puree. With the machine running, drizzle in the oils in a slow, steady stream in order to emulsify and get creamy. Fold in the fresh parsley and season with salt and pepper.

Simple Local Lettuce Salad

Sometimes salad can be over the top with too many ingredients. I love this recipe because it's simple and just lets the salad take center stage. But make no mistake—you can taste each and every vegetable. That is why I love this salad so much.

◆ **Makes 4 large salads** ◆

Black Pepper Croutons

4 cups (140 g) crustless brioche or other soft bread, cut into ½-inch (12-mm) cubes

¾ cup (170 g) unsalted butter, melted

1 tbsp (8 g) minced garlic

1½ tsp (3 g) ground black pepper, or less if you want it milder

Salt, to taste

Salad

1 lb (454 g) local baby lettuce

⅓ cup (79 ml) Red Onion Vinaigrette (page 112)

Salt and pepper, to taste

¼ cup (29 g) peeled and julienned watermelon radish

¼ cup (56 g) crumbled goat cheese

1 cup (120 g) seeded and sliced English cucumber

¼ cup (40 g) thinly sliced red onion

¼ cup (32 g) carrots, cut into matchsticks

Preheat the oven to 400°F (204°C). Toss together the bread cubes, melted butter, garlic, black pepper and salt and spread in an even layer on a baking sheet. Toast in the oven until golden brown, about 4 to 5 minutes.

Place the lettuce in a large salad bowl and toss with the Red Onion Vinaigrette and 1 cup (35 g) of croutons (save the rest for another time). Season with salt and pepper. Top with the radish, goat cheese, cucumber, red onion and carrots and serve immediately.

Baby Spinach Salad

This salad is like the perfect marriage of ingredients. They are all connected as if they were best friends. Cheddar goes with apple, apple goes with maple, maple goes with pecans and ham goes with spinach. You follow me?

 Serves 4

8 paper-thin slices aged country ham (or prosciutto)

8 oz (227 g) baby spinach leaves

1 Granny Smith apple, cut into matchsticks

½ cup (118 ml) Maple Vinaigrette (page 113)

2 radishes, sliced thin

4 oz (113 g) cheddar, crumbled (Coastal Farms brand or other crumbly cheddar)

½ cup (55 g) toasted pecans

Line plates with the ham. Then, in a mixing bowl, combine the baby spinach and apple with the Maple Vinaigrette and place atop the ham. Top with the sliced radishes, crumbled cheddar and toasted pecans.

Red Onion Vinaigrette

This vinaigrette was the first thing I learned when I was hired at Tremont 647 back in 1996. I have been using this recipe ever since and it remains unchanged because it is that good. Every time I serve a salad with this vinaigrette everybody always asks for the recipe.

◆ Makes about 2½ cups (593 ml) ◆

1 medium red onion, roughly chopped

2 cloves garlic

2 tbsp (30 ml) Dijon mustard

2 tbsp (3 g) fresh rosemary leaves

1 tbsp (4 g) fresh parsley leaves

2 tsp (10 ml) honey

¼ cup (59 ml) red wine vinegar

¼ cup (59 ml) balsamic vinegar

1½ cups (355 ml) blended oil

Salt and pepper, to taste

In a blender, add the red onion, garlic, Dijon mustard, herbs, honey and vinegars. Puree until smooth, then slowly drizzle in the oil to emulsify. Season with salt and pepper. Store in the refrigerator for up to 2 weeks.

MAPLE VINAIGRETTE

This is such a great fall vinaigrette that is so smooth in flavor and versatile, too—it's not just a salad dressing. DO NOT substitute Aunt Jemima or I will come for you!

◆ MAKES 3 CUPS (710 ML) ◆

2 cups (475 ml) mayonnaise

¼ cup (59 ml) balsamic vinegar

¼ cup (59 ml) Vermont maple syrup

¼ cup (59 ml) Dijon mustard

¼ cup (59 ml) water

Salt and pepper, to taste

Whisk together the mayonnaise, vinegar, maple syrup, mustard and water and season with salt and pepper. Store in the refrigerator for up to 2 weeks.

SUGAR COATED

In my opinion, you cannot have a complete meal without having at least a bite of something sweet at the end. I am not a pastry chef by any means, but because of that I have made these desserts both relatively simple and very fun to eat. The recipes in this chapter are Southern staples that any good Cajun cook should have in their repertoire. Make them, love them, share them!

Fresh Fried Beignets

One word . . . fried pillow of love. Okay, that's four words, but if you come to the bayou and don't have a beignet, you are not human. Lucky for you, you can now make these babies at home, too.

◆ ◆ **SERVES 6 TO 8** ◆ ◆

Beignets

1½ cups (355 ml) warm water (100–105°F [38–41°C])

2 packets active dry yeast

½ cup (100 g) granulated sugar

1 tsp salt

1 tsp cayenne

2 large eggs

1 cup (237 ml) evaporated milk

8 cups (960 g) all-purpose flour, plus more as needed, divided

4 tbsp (52 g) bacon fat

Butter, for greasing

Canola oil, for deep frying

2 cups (250 g) powdered sugar mixed with 1 tsp ground cinnamon

Vanilla Bean Cream

2 cups (465 g) mascarpone cheese

1 vanilla bean, scraped

2 tbsp (25 g) granulated sugar

¼ cup (59 ml) heavy cream

For the beignets, in a stand mixer with the dough hook attached, add the warm water, yeast and sugar. Mix gently and then let sit for 10 to 12 minutes or until it foams. In a separate bowl, whisk together the salt, cayenne, eggs and evaporated milk. With the mixer on low, add the egg mixture to the yeast mixture. Add half of the flour and mix until just combined. Add the bacon fat, and then gradually add the remaining flour until a dough forms. Remove the dough from the bowl, place it on a lightly floured surface and knead it until smooth.

Place the dough in a large buttered bowl and cover with plastic wrap. Let the dough rest someplace warm for at least 2 to 3 hours, or overnight in the refrigerator. Once rested, place the dough onto a lightly floured surface. Dust with flour as needed. Roll the dough out to about ¼ inch (6 mm) thick and cut into 12 to 16 squares. Place the squares on a butter-greased baking pan, cover with plastic wrap and let sit for 15 minutes at room temperature until they rise again.

In a large, heavy-bottomed pot or cast-iron pan, heat the oil to 350°F (177°C). Fry the beignets in batches, turning constantly until they are evenly golden brown on both sides. Remove from the oil to a paper towel–lined platter. Hammer with cinnamon powdered sugar and serve immediately with the vanilla bean cream.

For the vanilla bean cream, whip the mascarpone, vanilla, sugar and cream until smooth and creamy.

Cast Iron Caramel Biscuit Pudding

Who doesn't love a slab of warm, sweet, gooey, rich bread pudding? Answer is no one, that's who! These flavors are astonishing together. This dessert is obviously best when warm, but because it's made in cast iron, you can make it ahead of time and then reheat it when you need it.

Serves 8 to 10

Bread Pudding

11 eggs, beaten

8 cups (2 L) milk

2 cups (475 ml) heavy cream

1½ tsp (4 g) cinnamon

1½ cups (300 g) sugar

2 tbsp (26 g) vanilla paste or 2 vanilla beans, scraped

Juice and zest of 1 orange

8 day-old Buttermilk & Bourbon's Honey-Glazed Biscuits (page 13), crumbled

2 tbsp (28 g) cold unsalted butter, for greasing the pan

2 cups (480 g) caramel chips

Root-Beer Whipped Cream

1 cup (237 ml) heavy whipping cream

¼ cup (31 g) powdered sugar, plus more for garnish

1 tsp vanilla extract

¼ tsp root beer extract

Bourbon Sauce

1 cup (200 g) granulated sugar

3 tbsp (45 ml) water

1 cup (237 ml) heavy cream

¼ cup (57 g) unsalted butter

Pinch of salt

2 tbsp (30 ml) bourbon

Plating

Vanilla ice cream, melted

Powdered sugar, for garnish

Mint, for garnish

For the bread pudding, preheat the oven to 350°F (177°C), then mix the eggs, milk, heavy cream, cinnamon, sugar, vanilla and orange juice and zest in a large bowl. Place the crumbled biscuits in a separate bowl. Pour the mixture over the biscuits and let sit for 15 minutes. Rub a 10- to 12-inch (25- to 30-cm) cast-iron pan with the butter and pour the mixture in. Top with the caramel chips. Cover with aluminum foil and bake for 40 minutes or until the middle is set.

To make the whipped cream, using a stand mixer with the whisk attachment, whip the heavy cream and powdered sugar on high for 1 to 2 minutes or until soft peaks have formed. Add the vanilla and root beer extracts and beat for about a minute longer, or until stiff peaks have formed.

To make the bourbon sauce, combine the sugar and water in a heavy-bottomed saucepan. Cook the sugar until it begins to change color. When it is a caramel color, remove from the heat and carefully whisk in the heavy cream, butter, salt and bourbon.

Serve the caramel bread pudding right in the cast-iron pan, or cut wedges and top with the root-beer whipped cream and spoon some melted ice cream and bourbon sauce over the top. Garnish with powdered sugar and mint.

Roasted Strawberry and Glazed doughnut milkshakes

You could seriously make some friends with this. This is not your average everyday milkshake, I assure you. Roasting the strawberries deepens the flavor and blending it with buttermilk gives it a nice tartness. Then add a glazed doughnut to the mix and your life has been transformed forever. Please mail thank-you cards to . . .

 MAKES 2

1 lb (454 g) strawberries, washed, trimmed and halved

¼ cup (59 ml) milk

¼ cup (59 ml) buttermilk

2–3 cups (264–396 g) vanilla ice cream, depending how thick you like it

3 honey-glazed doughnuts, divided

Whipped Cream (page 125)

Preheat the oven to 350°F (177°C). Spread the strawberries on a baking dish. Roast for 10 to 12 minutes, until the strawberries are soft and the juices begin to caramelize. Remove the strawberries from the oven and set aside to cool.

Once the strawberries are cool, add them to a blender along with the milk, buttermilk, ice cream and 2 of the doughnuts, broken into pieces. Blend on high until smooth.

Pour into tall milkshake glasses and garnish with Whipped Cream and the remaining doughnut split into two.

Warm Gingerbread Cake

I know gingerbread probably screams winter holidays, but honestly it is just a great tasting spiced cake that can be made any time of the year. This even goes together swimmingly with summer fruits.

Gingerbread Cake

2½ cups (300 g) all-purpose flour

1½ tsp (7 g) baking soda

½ tsp salt

½ tsp ground cinnamon

½ tsp ground ginger

½ tsp ground cloves

1 cup (227 g) unsalted butter

½ cup (100 g) granulated sugar

½ cup (118 ml) molasses

2 eggs

2 tsp (9 g) vanilla paste

1 cup (237 ml) boiling water

Maple–Fig (or Peach) Relish

2½ cups (385 g) fresh black Mission figs (or peaches), diced

½ cup (118 ml) pure maple syrup

Juice of 2 limes

1 tbsp (6 g) fresh ginger, peeled and minced

Candied Walnuts

1 egg white

1 tsp water

¼ cup (50 g) granulated sugar

3 tbsp (38 g) light brown sugar

½ tsp salt

½ tsp cinnamon, ground

½ tsp vanilla paste

2 cups (236 g) walnuts

Plating

Whipped Cream (page 125)

Mint sprigs, for garnish

Powdered sugar, for garnish

For the gingerbread, grease a 10-inch (25-cm) square pan. Preheat the oven to 325°F (163°C).

Mix the flour, baking soda, salt, cinnamon, ginger and cloves together and set aside. In a separate bowl, cream the butter, then gradually add the sugar and cream thoroughly. Stir in the molasses. Beat the eggs until thick and combine with the creamed mixture. Stir in the vanilla paste.

Add the dry ingredients to the creamed mixture a third at a time, mixing well after each addition. Gradually add the boiling water, stirring after each addition. Turn into the prepared pan. Bake for about 40 to 50 minutes until the cake is firm in the middle and a toothpick comes out clean.

For the relish, combine the figs (or peaches), maple syrup, lime juice and ginger and mix.

For the candied walnuts, preheat the oven to 225°F (107°C). Spray a baking sheet with nonstick spray. Whip the egg white until frothy, then mix with the water, sugar, brown sugar, salt, cinnamon, vanilla paste and walnuts. Spread the nut mixture onto the prepared baking sheet. Bake until the nuts are deep golden and the mixture is bubbling and dry looking, stirring occasionally to break up clumps, about 30 minutes. Cool completely on the baking sheet. The candied walnuts can be made up to 3 days ahead and stored in an airtight container.

To serve, place a piece of warm gingerbread on a plate and top with fruit relish, Whipped Cream and candied walnuts. Garnish with mint and powdered sugar.

Banana Cream Pie

Anybody that knows me knows I adore any kind of cream pie, but I hate making pie crusts. I usually just buy one when I am making this at home. I personally use a graham cracker crust, but any pie crust works just as well because it is honestly just the vehicle to put a little heaven into your mouth.

◆ **Makes one 9-inch (23-cm) pie** ◆

Pastry Cream

¾ cup (150 g) sugar

¼ cup (32 g) cornstarch

½ tsp salt

3 cups (710 ml) milk

3 egg yolks, slightly beaten

1 tbsp (14 g) unsalted butter

2 tsp (9 g) vanilla paste

Whipped Cream

1 cup (237 ml) heavy cream

½ tsp vanilla paste

2 tbsp (25 g) sugar

Assembly

3 ripe bananas, sliced into rounds

9-inch (23-cm) pie shell, homemade or store-bought

½ cup (66 g) chocolate shavings

In a heavy-bottomed saucepan, mix together the sugar, cornstarch, salt and milk. Heat over medium heat, stirring constantly to ensure scorching won't occur. When it starts to thicken, let it boil for 1 minute. Remove from the heat. With a ladle, slowly add the hot mixture to the egg yolks a little bit at a time while stirring constantly so the eggs don't curdle. When the eggs are tempered, add them back into the saucepan. Place the mixture back on the stove and simmer for 1 more minute until the pastry cream is the desired thickness. Remove from the heat and whisk in the butter and vanilla paste.

For the whipped cream, using a stand mixer, whip the heavy cream, vanilla paste and sugar until stiff peaks form.

To assemble the pie, place the sliced bananas in a single layer on the bottom of the pie shell of your choice and pour the pastry cream over them. Refrigerate for 1 hour, then spread whipped cream over the top. Sprinkle the chocolate shavings across the top and serve.

BOURBON HOT CHOCOLATE

I really have nothing to say about this recipe other than if I had a microphone, I would just drop it and walk away.

 SERVES 2

CHERRY JAM

2 tbsp (25 g) minced Luxardo cherries

1 tbsp (13 g) light brown sugar

1 tbsp (15 ml) cherry liqueur

HOT CHOCOLATE

2½ cups (593 ml) milk

2 cups (475 ml) half and half

½ vanilla bean, split

½ cinnamon stick

4 oz (113 g) dark chocolate, chopped

4 oz (113 g) milk chocolate, chopped

1 tbsp (8 g) powdered sugar

1 tsp instant espresso

¼ cup (59 ml) or more of bourbon

1 cup (132 g) marshmallow fluff

2 tsp (6 g) cocoa nibs

For the cherry jam, simmer the cherries, brown sugar and liqueur in a small pot until reduced and syrupy, about 8 to 10 minutes.

In a saucepan, bring the milk, half and half, vanilla bean and cinnamon stick to a simmer. Remove the pan from the heat and add both chocolates. When the chocolates are melted, add the powdered sugar and espresso powder and mix. Reheat gently, remove the vanilla bean and cinnamon stick and add bourbon to taste. Pour into mugs, top with marshmallow fluff, torch until slightly burned, then top with cocoa nibs and cherry jam.

Warm Butterscotch Fondant

A fondant is a *petit gâteau*, French for "small cake." This recipe was my signature dessert when I was the chef at Gargoyles in Davis Square in Somerville back in the day. It is unbelievably heavenly. This was also the dessert I served at the James Beard House. This is similar to those rich chocolate flourless cakes that you see everywhere, but this one has butterscotch and a little flour. Way cooler!

◆ ▰ MAKES 8 CAKES ▰ ◆

CRÈME ANGLAISE

6 egg yolks

½ cup (100 g) granulated sugar

2 cups (475 ml) heavy cream

¼ cup (26 g) chicory coffee beans (I prefer Café Du Monde brand), crushed

BUTTERSCOTCH FONDANTS

10 tbsp (142 g) unsalted butter

8 oz (227 g) butterscotch chips

5 eggs

½ cup (113 g) light brown sugar

½ cup (100 g) granulated sugar

2 tbsp (30 ml) butterscotch schnapps

¾ cup plus 2 tbsp (105 g) all-purpose flour, divided

MACERATED STRAWBERRIES

16 strawberries, quartered

1 tbsp (13 g) granulated sugar

1 vanilla bean, scraped

To make the crème anglaise, starting in a medium-size mixing bowl, whisk together the egg yolks and sugar until they are very pale yellow and smooth. In a medium-size saucepan, bring to a boil the heavy cream and coffee. Whisk about half the cream mixture into the egg yolks until well combined, then pour back into the saucepan. Over medium heat, stirring constantly with a wooden spoon, cook until the mixture heavily coats the back of the spoon. Don't scramble the eggs. Strain into a clean bowl and set the bowl over ice cubes and cold water until chilled, stirring occasionally. Refrigerate, covered, until needed.

To make the fondants, preheat the oven to 325°F (163°C). Melt the butter with the butterscotch chips in a small pot. Meanwhile, in a stand mixer using the whip attachment, beat the eggs and both sugars until they are very pale yellow and smooth. Add the butterscotch mixture to the mixer. Add the butterscotch schnapps and ¾ cup (90 g) of flour just until combined, being careful not to over-mix. Coat the insides of 8 (4-ounce [118-ml]) ramekins with cooking spray, then dust with the remaining 2 tablespoons (15 g) flour. Bake for 12 to 15 minutes. Let the fondants cool slightly, then flip out of ramekins.

For the strawberries, mix together the strawberries, sugar and vanilla and serve immediately.

Serve the fondants warm topped with the macerated strawberries and crème anglaise.

ADULT BEVERAGES

New Orleans is a party town and as crazy as it can get as far as the cocktails go. It is generally known for classics like The Hurricane or The Crusta. I certainly appreciate them, but I am not a classic type guy, so I want to push you a little to be more creative with the drinks. I think besides technique, creativity is the difference between a bartender and a full-blown mixologist. I am giving you some old-school and new-school flavors for you to try. So you can decide—are you classic or creative?

Boston-Nola Hurricane

When I say "New Orleans" you say "Hurricane!" When I say "New Orleans" you say "Hurricane!" Catch my drift? This is THE drink of New Orleans. The only difference between my recipe and what you would find in New Orleans is about 2 pounds of sugar in each drink. This is still a sweet drink for sure, but my version tastes even better because we replace some of that sugar with a lot more flavor. This will definitely transport you to Bourbon Street . . . and maybe a night of drunken debauchery.

Makes 1

Simple Syrup

2 tbsp (30 ml) boiling water

2 tbsp (25 g) granulated sugar

Cocktail

1 oz (30 ml) dark rum

1 oz (30 ml) light rum

1 oz (30 ml) orange juice

½ oz (15 ml) grenadine

½ oz (15 ml) lime juice

¾ oz (23 ml) pineapple juice

¼ oz (7 ml) passion fruit juice

1 orange slice, for garnish

1 maraschino cherry, for garnish

For the simple syrup, combine the water and sugar and stir until the sugar dissolves.

For the cocktail, in a mixing glass filled with ice, combine both rums, the orange juice, grenadine, lime juice, ½ ounce (15 ml) of simple syrup, pineapple juice and passion fruit juice and shake.

Strain over fresh ice. Garnish with an orange slice and a maraschino cherry.

WHO DAT?

James Patterson is my bar manager and master mixologist at Buttermilk & Bourbon. He has been with me from the beginning, and without him Buttermilk would not be what we are today. This is one of his favorite fall drinks that we serve because it's very refreshing but has a deep, full-bodied sweet and sour flavor. And James just happens to be a New Orleans Saints Fan.

MAKES 1

Rich Simple Syrup

2 tbsp (30 ml) boiling water

4 tbsp (50 g) granulated sugar

Cocktail

1 egg white

3 raspberries

1 oz (30 ml) lemon juice

1 dash chocolate-mole bitters

2 oz (60 ml) rye whiskey (I use Old Overholt Bottled in Bond)

For the simple syrup, combine the boiling water and sugar and stir until the sugar is dissolved and let cool.

In a mixing glass, combine the egg white, raspberries, 1 ounce (30 ml) simple syrup, lemon juice and bitters and dry shake for 60 seconds. Add the whiskey and ice, then shake for an additional minute. Strain and serve in a coupe glass. No garnish necessary.

NOTE: I always use fresh lemon juice. You can buy it but make sure it's 100 percent pure lemon juice and it absolutely doesn't come in a plastic lemon.

Garden District

This is a very well-balanced cocktail with a great strawberry taste and a nice gingersnap ending. Maker's Mark is a very soft bourbon, so this makes it an easy sipping drink especially if you have a front porch on a bayou to just watch the alligators go by.

Makes 1

Honey-Strawberry Syrup

1½ tbsp (23 ml) honey

¼ cup (59 ml) water

¼ cup (50 g) granulated sugar

8 strawberries

Cocktail

2 oz (60 ml) bourbon (Maker's Mark preferred)

1 oz (30 ml) lemon juice

1 (12-oz [355-ml]) can ginger beer

1 lemon wheel

For the honey-strawberry syrup, simmer the honey, water, sugar and strawberries in a small saucepan until the strawberries become very mushy, about 8 to 10 minutes. Puree and strain. This will keep for a few weeks refrigerated.

For the cocktail, combine the bourbon, ½ ounce (15 ml) of honey-strawberry syrup and lemon juice in a shaker and shake. Strain over fresh ice. Top with the ginger beer and garnish with a lemon wheel.

The Marie Laveau

Marie Laveau was a renowned practitioner of voodoo in New Orleans in the late 1800s. It's said that over ten thousand people swarmed the shore of Lake Pontchartrain just to catch a glimpse of her performing these legendary rites. This is me respecting her legend and lore.

MAKES 1

2 oz (60 ml) amber cognac (I prefer Pierre Ferrand)

1 oz (30 ml) Lillet

1 oz (30 ml) elderflower liqueur (I prefer St. Germain)

1 oz (30 ml) lychee puree

Splash of champagne or prosecco

Champagne grapes on the vine, for garnish

In a shaker, combine the cognac, Lillet and elderflower liqueur with the lychee puree. Shake and strain into a glass and top with champagne or prosecco.

Garnish with the champagne grapes with some in and some out of the glass, creating a very sexy look.

VOODOO ON THE BAYOU

This is a take on the classic New Orleans cocktail called the Crusta. This is a very fall cocktail geared to warm you up. Don't let the ingredients scare you off—it is worth the extra effort.

MAKES 1

Orange-Cinnamon Oleo Saccharum

2 oranges' worth of peels

2 tbsp (25 g) sugar

Cinnamon sticks or ¼ tsp ground cinnamon, to taste

Cocktail

1¾ oz (52 ml) bourbon (I prefer Old Forrester)

¼ oz (7 ml) lemon juice

½ oz (15 ml) cherry liqueur (I like Cherry Heering)

1 dash Angostura bitters

To make the oleo saccharum, mix and marinate the peels and sugar overnight and use as is or dilute with hot water, up to 2 tablespoons (30 ml), to make a syrup. Leave a stick of cinnamon to macerate in the mixture overnight. Optionally, you can stir in up to ¼ teaspoon of ground cinnamon, to taste.

In a mixing glass with ice, combine the bourbon, ³/₄ ounce (23 ml) of oleo saccharum syrup, lemon juice, cherry liqueur and bitters and stir 20 to 30 turns or until chilled. Then strain and serve in a cordial glass.

Beautiful Liar

This cocktail is one of the prettiest summer cocktails I have ever had. You don't necessarily think of tequila with New Orleans, but you do think of craft cocktails, and tequila is on the upswing, so I am just getting you ahead of the curve. Plus I have had a lot of these while doing research, testing recipes and now writing this book, so that makes it extra, extra Southern, right?

Makes 1

Cherry-Infused Tequila

40 fresh cherries

1 (750-ml) bottle of tequila

Cocktail

½ oz (15 ml) honey

2 dashes orange flower water

1 oz (30 ml) fresh lime juice

½ oz (15 ml) orange liqueur (I prefer Bauchant)

2 tsp (12 g) black lava salt

1 lime wheel

To infuse the tequila, first wash the cherries well and then remove the pits. Place the cherries in a glass container with the tequila and allow to infuse for a minimum of 2 days but up to 2 weeks. Remove the fruit when ready and strain.

In a shaker, combine ice, honey, orange flower water, lime juice, orange liqueur and 2 ounces (60 ml) of infused tequila. Shake and pour over fresh crushed ice in a rock glass rimmed with black lava salt. Garnish with a lime wheel.

Cajun Bloody Mary

As a chef, you are always trying to get better. Sometimes that means changing recipes, adjusting and rethinking, but not for this recipe. I have been using this for over a decade and haven't changed it or even wanted to. Traditionally I use vodka here, but you could also use tequila, gin or whiskey as well. This is so good you can drink it without the booze in it, and that is saying something!

Makes 8

Cajun Bloody Mary Mix

3 cups (710 ml) tomato juice

½ tsp minced parsley

2 tbsp (30 ml) Worcestershire sauce

2 tbsp (30 ml) apple cider vinegar

2 tbsp (30 ml) molasses

2 tbsp (30 ml) hot sauce

1 tbsp (15 ml) pickle juice

¼ cup (60 g) prepared horseradish

½ tsp salt

½ tsp House Cajun Spice (page 155)

¼ tsp red pepper flakes

1/8 tsp chili powder

1/8 tsp ground cloves

½ tsp granulated garlic

¼ tsp onion powder

¼ tsp oregano

1/8 tsp thyme

¼ tsp black pepper

Cocktail

1 cup (237 ml) Okra Vegetable Vodka (page 146)

House Cajun Spice (page 155), for rimming the glasses

Lemon wedge, to garnish, optional

Celery sticks, to garnish, optional

Pickled okra, to garnish, optional

Lemon Shandy–Poached Peel-and-Eat Shrimp (page 76), to garnish, optional

Olives, to garnish, optional

Bacon strips, to garnish, optional

Pickles, to garnish, optional

To make the Bloody Mary mix, combine the tomato juice, parsley, Worcestershire sauce, vinegar, molasses, hot sauce, pickle juice, horseradish, salt, House Cajun Spice, red pepper flakes, chili powder, ground cloves, granulated garlic, onion powder, oregano, thyme and black pepper and refrigerate for at least a few hours but preferably longer. This will keep for 2 weeks or more in the fridge.

In a shaker with ice, combine the vegetable vodka and 4 cups (1 L) of Bloody Mary mix. Strain over fresh ice in a pint glass rimmed with House Cajun Spice and garnish it with a lemon wedge, celery sticks, pickled okra, poached shrimp, olives, bacon strips, pickles, a cheeseburger, lobster tail, your flip flop, couch cushion, a dozen doughnuts, etc. Get what I am saying? Use whatever you like and be creative—you won't hurt my feelings!

Okra Vegetable Vodka

I have been drinking this recipe in one way or another for a very long time. When I was researching brunches in New Orleans I saw many different variations of infusions. I like a lot of okra flavor in mine and it's a great way to incorporate a nice vegetable flavor for Cajun Bloody Marys, martinis or any other savory cocktail.

Makes 24 servings (enough for one Sunday brunch . . . hopefully)

1 clove garlic

½ lb (227 g) okra

1 stalk celery

½ green bell pepper, seeded and cut

1 medium-size tomato, halved

½ cup (75 g) thick-sliced Spanish onions

1 (1.75-L) bottle vodka

$\frac{1}{8}$ tsp red pepper flakes

$\frac{1}{8}$ tsp whole black peppercorns

1 bay leaf

Preheat the broiler to high. Place the garlic, okra, celery, bell pepper, tomato and onion in a baking dish and broil until the vegetables are slightly charred with some nice color, about 5 minutes. Combine the broiled vegetables with the vodka, red pepper flakes, peppercorns and bay leaf and let sit for 1 week.

Lagniappe

In New Orleans a lagniappe (pronounced LAN-yap) means a little something extra. You might not necessarily find this version there, but I believe this is an exciting cocktail that captures the spirit of the city and makes you a little bit extra when you drink one, two—no more than five. Treat yourself!

Makes 1

Strawberry Shrub

1 cup (166 g) strawberries, sliced
1 cup (200 g) sugar
1 cup (237 ml) red wine vinegar

Banana Syrup

½ banana, peeled and sliced
1 cup (200 g) sugar
1 cup (237 ml) water

Cocktail

2 oz (60 ml) agricole rum
¾ oz (23 ml) lemon juice
2 dashes 'Elemakule Tiki® Bitters
Pinch of sea salt
Fresh strawberry, for garnish

To make the strawberry shrub, combine the strawberries, sugar and red wine vinegar in a small saucepan over low heat and mash the berries to release as much juice as possible, then stir until the sugar is dissolved. Refrigerate overnight. The next day, heat gently over low heat, just until the sugar is dissolved but not simmered. Strain through a fine sieve.

To make the banana syrup, combine the banana, sugar and water in a small saucepan and simmer until the sugar is dissolved. Remove from the heat and refrigerate overnight, then strain through a fine sieve.

To make the cocktail, combine the rum, ½ ounce (15 ml) of strawberry shrub, ½ ounce (15 ml) of banana syrup, lemon juice, bitters and sea salt in a shaker with ice and shake vigorously.

Strain into a highball glass over crushed ice. Stir with a bar spoon and garnish with a fresh strawberry.

BRINES, RUBS, SEASONINGS & MARINADES

These recipes are like the support staff in a restaurant (dishwashers, food runners, bar-backs, bussers, etc.). Yes, you could try to pull it off without them, but it wouldn't be pretty. Agree? Good. This chapter is all about making good food great. It's about adding flavor and also a little insurance that we are supporting the main ingredient as much as we can. For instance, when you come to Buttermilk and get our fried chicken (which is delicious by itself), you also have an option to have it rubbed with Nashville Hot Spice (page 157), immersed in a Sweet and Spicy Glaze (page 158), drizzled with Jalapeño BBQ Syrup (page 158) or topped with White BBQ Sauce (page 151). Get what I'm saying?

White BBQ Sauce

This is maybe my favorite recipe in this book. I put this sh*t on everything! This is the most popular sauce at the restaurant and all of my staff call this "crack sauce" because it is literally good on anything. Use it as a marinade or a BBQ sauce or a salad dressing or a dipping sauce.

◆ ❰ Makes about 4 cups (1 L) ❱ ◆

2 cups (475 ml) mayonnaise

2 tbsp (30 g) prepared horseradish

2 tbsp (30 ml) water

4 tbsp (28 g) black pepper, coarse grind

2 tbsp (30 ml) whole grain mustard

3 tbsp (30 g) granulated garlic

¼ cup (59 ml) cider vinegar

¼ cup (59 ml) lemon juice

¼ cup (55 g) light brown sugar

¼ tsp cayenne pepper

¼ tsp ground cumin

¼ tsp chili powder

2 tsp (10 ml) Worcestershire sauce

Mix together the mayonnaise, horseradish, water, black pepper, mustard, granulated garlic, vinegar, lemon juice, brown sugar, cayenne pepper, cumin, chili powder and Worcestershire sauce. This mixture will keep, refrigerated, for up to 2 weeks.

House Brine

There are a million types of brines out there, but they are all basically the same base; salt, sugar and water. This is a great all-purpose flavored brine that we use daily for pork and chicken. I am a big fan of brining; it's essentially moisture insurance so that even if you don't cook the protein perfectly, it will still be moist. All you need to do is make sure the liquid covers the protein entirely and keep it in the brine at least 12 hours but not more than 24.

◆ Makes about 8 cups (2 L), or enough brine for up to 5 pounds (2.3 kg) of protein ◆

¼ cup (72 g) salt

¾ cup (177 ml) honey

4 cups (1 L) boiling water

½ Granny Smith apple, quartered

½ onion, roughly chopped

½ carrot, roughly chopped

1 stalk celery, roughly chopped

1 tsp dried thyme leaves

2 fresh sage leaves

2 tsp (6 g) whole black peppercorns

2 cups (281 g) ice

In a large bowl, mix the salt, honey and hot water. Add the apple, onion, carrot, celery, thyme, sage and peppercorns. Add the ice to cool the brine. Add your protein and let it sit, refrigerated, for 12 to 24 hours depending on the thickness. Remove from the brine and pat dry before cooking.

Apple Cider Brine

This is probably my favorite brine to date. It has such a deep flavor with an enjoyable touch of sweetness. This brine definitely gives you a serious apple taste, so make sure you are looking for that—otherwise use the House Brine (page 152).

◆ **Makes about 8 cups (2 L), or enough for up to 5 pounds (2.3 kg) of protein** ◆

¾ cup (216 g) salt

¾ cup (150 g) sugar

2 cups (475 ml) apple cider

1 tsp red pepper flakes

1 bay leaf

½ cup (67 g) garlic cloves

2 tbsp (5 g) dried thyme

½ tsp cinnamon, ground

1 small white onion, julienned

4 cups (1 L) very hot water

Mix the salt, sugar, apple cider, red pepper flakes, bay leaf, garlic, thyme, cinnamon and onion. Then add the hot water and mix until the salt and sugar are dissolved. Chill the brine until cool, then add your protein and let sit in the refrigerator overnight.

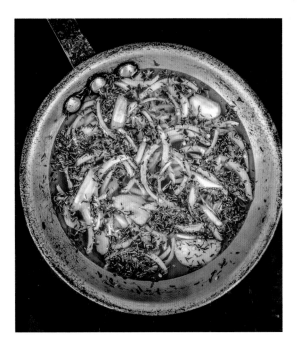

AKA RUB

United States Marines have the Rifleman's Creed as part as their doctrine. I have written my own dogma about this rub:

This is my meat rub. There are many like it, but this one is mine. It is my life. I must master it as I must master my life. Without me, my rub is useless. Without my rub, I am useless. I must use my rub true. I must cook better than the enemy who is trying to outcook me. I must outcook him before he outcooks me. My rub and I know that what counts in cooking is not the food we cook, the noise of our burst or the smoke we make. We know that it is the taste that counts. We will taste. My rub is almost human, even as I am human, because it is my life. I will learn its weaknesses, its strengths, its parts, its flavors, its heat and its value. I will keep my rub dry and ready, even as I am ready. We will become part of each other. We will . . .

◆ MAKES ABOUT 3 CUPS (500 G) ◆

½ cup (113 g) light brown sugar

½ cup (100 g) granulated sugar

½ cup (54 g) paprika

½ cup (144 g) salt

¼ cup (24 g) ground cumin

¼ cup (28 g) ground black pepper

2 tbsp (16 g) chili powder

2 tbsp (19 g) garlic powder

2 tbsp (14 g) onion powder

1 tbsp (6 g) mustard powder

1 tsp dried thyme

1 tsp red pepper flakes

1 tsp cayenne

¼ tsp Old Bay seasoning

Whisk together the brown sugar, granulated sugar, paprika, salt, cumin, black pepper, chili powder, garlic powder, onion powder, mustard powder, thyme, red pepper flakes, cayenne and Old Bay and rub on any meat before cooking. This has a ton of flavor and will give you a nice brown crust. This will keep dry up to a month.

House Cajun Spice

This is pretty much the base of everything New Orleans as far as spice goes. I use it a lot in this book and it's a great way to give your food a nice punch. All chefs have their own version, and after plenty of testing, this is ours.

½ cup (54 g) paprika

½ cup (17 g) dried basil

½ cup (22 g) dried thyme

¼ cup (24 g) filé gumbo powder

2 tbsp (16 g) chili powder

½ tsp cayenne

1 tsp ground bay leaves

Mix the paprika, basil, thyme, filé, chili powder, cayenne and bay leaves and keep dry for up to a month.

CORRUPTION SPICE

First and foremost, this is not to be confused with a member of the Spice Girls! This is a spice rub, not a dry rub, and you shouldn't use a ton of this. This is for seasoning only. We use this in our Sweet and Spicy Glaze (page 158), but you can also use it to jack up the seasoning of anything. The cinnamon adds a nice unique touch of flavor, but could be overpowering if used recklessly. So tell me what you want what you really really want.

◆ Makes about 2 cups (320 g) ◆

½ cup (78 g) garlic powder

½ cup (64 g) chili powder

¼ cup (72 g) salt

¼ cup (50 g) sugar

¼ cup (27 g) paprika

4 tsp (9 g) celery salt

4 tsp (11 g) lemon pepper

4 tsp (10 g) ground cinnamon

Mix the garlic powder, chili powder, salt, sugar, paprika, celery salt, lemon pepper and cinnamon and keep dry for up to a month.

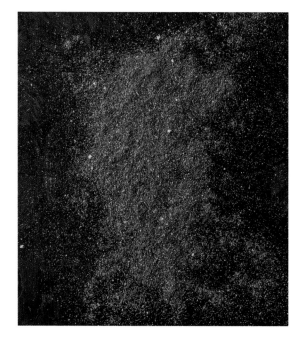

Nashville Hot Spice

It's hot but delicious, and you can use as little or as much as you want. This is not just for hot Nashville chicken. It's a good general spicy seasoning when you want to up your heat game for anything, but beware: It definitely packs some heat!

◆ MAKES 2 CUPS (300 G) ◆

1 cup (85 g) cayenne
¼ cup (72 g) salt
⅓ cup (33 g) dry mustard powder
3 tbsp (38 g) sugar
3 tbsp (20 g) smoked paprika
3 tbsp (21 g) ground black pepper
2 tbsp (20 g) granulated garlic

Mix the cayenne, salt, mustard powder, sugar, smoked paprika, black pepper and granulated garlic and keep dry for up to a month.

Sweet and Spicy Glaze

I like the combination of sweet and sour here, but with a completely different flavor profile than you're probably used to. This is a great sauce to actually just dip something right in. It coats perfectly. You can also drizzle over anything where you kind of want that sweet and sour taste. But be creative and glaze away.

◆ Makes 3¼ cups (769 ml) ◆

1 cup (237 ml) red wine vinegar

1 cup (237 ml) hot sauce (I prefer Crystal brand)

¼ cup (40 g) Corruption Spice (page 156)

2 cups (475 ml) honey

Combine the vinegar, hot sauce, Corruption Spice and honey in a small saucepan and bring to a boil. Remove from the heat. Serve warm. This will keep refrigerated for a few weeks.

*See photo on right.

Jalapeño BBQ Syrup

I feel like all BBQ sauces are just so cloyingly sweet and they all kind of taste the same. This recipe has way less sugar and far more tang than something that you would normally buy.

◆ Makes about 4 cups (1 L) ◆

1 jalapeño, stem removed and split

1¼ cups (296 ml) molasses

6 tbsp (89 ml) hoisin sauce

2 tbsp (30 ml) Dijon mustard

1 cup plus 2 tbsp (266 ml) ketchup

½ cup (118 ml) apple cider vinegar

½ cup (118 ml) honey

2 tsp (7 g) granulated garlic

2 tbsp (30 ml) tamarind concentrate

In a small pot, whisk the jalapeño, molasses, hoisin, mustard, ketchup, vinegar, honey, granulated garlic and tamarind and bring to a boil. Reduce the heat and simmer for 5 minutes. Remove from the heat and strain through a fine sieve. This will keep for a few weeks refrigerated.

Buffalo Sauce

Lisa Gauntt, a chef who worked for me for a long time, came up with this recipe, and I have used it ever since. Using some of the hot sauce along with other ingredients gives this recipe the familiar taste that we love but with a real homemade and unique flavor. This is also a great table hot sauce that can be used for basting on the grill or for a spicy dipping sauce.

◆ ❬ **Makes about 4 cups (1 L)** ❭ ◆

2 cups (300 g) julienned onions

3 cloves garlic, smashed

2 cups (454 g) unsalted butter, divided

1 tbsp (8 g) chili powder

1 tbsp (7 g) paprika

2 tsp (4 g) ground cumin

¼ cup (59 ml) dry white wine

1½ cups (355 ml) hot sauce

7 tbsp (85 g) light brown sugar

Water, as needed

1 tbsp (15 ml) honey

Salt and pepper, to taste

In a medium-size pot, sweat the onions and the garlic in 1 cup (227 g) of the butter until soft but with no color. Add the chili powder, paprika and cumin and cook for 30 seconds in order to release the natural oils.

Deglaze with the white wine and then add the hot sauce and light brown sugar and simmer on low heat for 15 minutes.

Remove from the heat and then in batches carefully puree in the blender with the remaining 1 cup (227 g) of butter until creamy, adding water until you have the desired consistency. Add the honey and season to taste with salt and pepper.

Carolina Gold Sauce

I like this sauce because it's sweet but still very tangy and has a nice viscosity that makes it perfect as a glaze or even a nice dipping sauce. Whatever you do, do not use Dijon mustard in place of the cheap yellow mustard; it's a completely different animal.

◆ **Makes about 2½ cups (593 ml)** ◆

1 cup (237 ml) apple cider vinegar

1 cup (237 ml) honey

¼ cup (59 ml) pure Vermont maple syrup

¼ cup (59 ml) dark molasses

1½ tsp (1 g) fresh thyme leaves or ½ tsp dried thyme

1½ cups (355 ml) cheap yellow mustard

1½ tsp (9 g) salt

¾ tsp red pepper flakes

½ tsp nutmeg

½ cup (75 g) grated onion

In a saucepan, combine the vinegar, honey, maple syrup, molasses, thyme, mustard, salt, red pepper flakes and nutmeg and bring to a simmer. Remove from the heat and mix in the onion. Serve hot or cold. This can be refrigerated for up to 2 weeks.

Buttermilk Marinade

This is pretty much what we soak everything in at the restaurant before we dredge and fry it. The buttermilk helps tenderize and add acidity and the hot sauce adds some tang but very little heat.

4 cups (1 L) buttermilk

1 cup (237 ml) hot sauce

1 tbsp (7 g) House Cajun Spice (page 155)

Mix together the buttermilk, hot sauce and House Cajun Spice. Keep refrigerated for up to a week.

Signature Fry Dredge

We use this as the base for all of our frying. Instead of cornmeal, we use masa flour, commonly used to make tortillas. The masa gives it such a great texture and adds a unique nuttiness to the dredge. You should keep about 50 pounds of this on hand at all times.

◆━ MAKES ABOUT 9 CUPS (1 KG) ━◆

4 cups (456 g) masa harina

4 cups (480 g) all-purpose flour

1 tbsp (9 g) lemon pepper

2 tbsp (20 g) granulated garlic

4 tsp (24 g) salt

2 tsp (8 g) Creole seasoning (I prefer Zatarain's)

2 tsp (5 g) ground black pepper

1 tsp red pepper flakes

1 tsp dried oregano

½ tsp cayenne pepper

Mix the masa flour, all-purpose flour, lemon pepper, granulated garlic, salt, Creole seasoning, black pepper, red pepper flakes, oregano and cayenne and keep dry for up to a month.

THINGS YOU SHOULD ALSO KNOW

These are some things I thought you should know; they are the essentials or accompaniments to other recipes in this book, as well as basics that will help you on your culinary journey. If they don't have a place now, they will soon, and you will use them often or I have not done a good job.

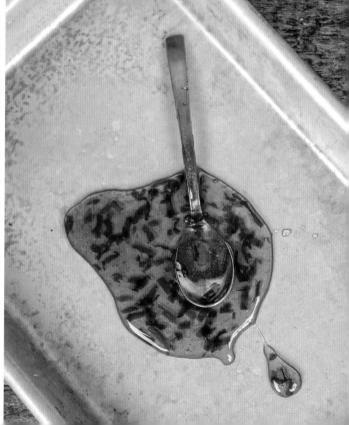

Infused Honeys

This is something exceptional yet standard to keep in a good Southern pantry. This honey is great for a variety of things: biscuits, fruit, cheese, etc. The list is endless.

Chile–Garlic Honey (Makes 2½ cups [593 ml])

2 cups (475 ml) honey

½ cup (118 ml) Asian chili paste (sambal oelek)

Juice of 1 lime

1 tsp granulated garlic

Black Truffle Honey (Makes 2½ cups [593 ml])

2 cups (475 ml) honey

½ cup (96 g) canned black truffle peelings, chopped

1 tsp salt

1 tbsp (15 ml) white truffle oil

Lemon–Rosemary Honey (Makes about 2 cups [475 ml])

2 cups (475 ml) honey

1 tbsp (2 g) fresh rosemary leaves

Zest and juice of 1 lemon

½ tsp lemon pepper

For the Chile–Garlic Honey

Combine the honey, chili paste, lime juice and granulated garlic in a small saucepan and bring to a boil, then remove from the heat. When cool store at room temperature for up to a month.

*See photo top right.

For the Black Truffle Honey

Combine the honey, truffle peelings and salt in a small saucepan. Bring to a boil, then remove from the heat. Add the truffle oil and when cool store at room temperature for up to a month.

*See photo bottom right.

For the Lemon–Rosemary Honey

Combine the honey, rosemary, lemon zest and juice and lemon pepper in a small saucepan. Bring to a boil, then remove from the heat. Once cool store at room temperature for up to a month.

*See photo far left.

Pimento Cheese

I love this stuff, it's no secret that mayonnaise is my favorite condiment of all time. So, mayonnaise pureed with roasted pimento peppers and cheese is life changing. Serve this with the Buttermilk & Bourbon's Honey-Glazed Biscuits (page 13), put it on a grilled cheese, a piece of grilled steak or a baked potato or just serve on Pepper Jack Crackers (page 65).

◆ Makes about 4 cups (550 g) ◆

4 oz (113 g) cream cheese, room temperature

¼ cup (65 g) diced jarred drained pimentos or roasted peppers

½ cup (118 ml) mayonnaise

1 cup (113 g) shredded yellow cheddar

1 cup (113 g) shredded pepper Jack cheese

1 tsp hot sauce

1 tsp smoked paprika

½ tsp garlic powder

½ tsp onion powder

2 tbsp (20 g) grated Spanish onion

Salt and pepper, to taste

Combine the cream cheese, pimentos, mayonnaise, cheddar, pepper Jack, hot sauce, paprika, garlic powder, onion powder, onion, salt and pepper in a food processor and puree until the mixture is slightly smooth but still has texture. Cover and keep refrigerated for up to a week.

Boiled Peanuts, Cheater's Version

You will find boiled peanuts on the side of the road everywhere in the South. These have virtually the same flavor but are much easier to make considering you don't need to shell them. Makes a great snack or use as the basis of Boiled Peanut Hummus (page 49).

◆ **Makes 4 cups (625 g)** ◆

8 cups (2 L) water

4 cups (584 g) roasted peanuts, shelled

2 tbsp (24 g) Creole seasoning (I prefer Zatarain's)

1 jalapeño, split in half

2 tsp (6 g) garlic powder

2 tbsp (14 g) House Cajun Spice (page 155)

½ tsp red pepper flakes

In a medium-size pot, combine the water, peanuts, Creole spice, jalapeño, garlic powder, House Cajun Spice and red pepper flakes and simmer until the peanuts are soft, adding more water if necessary. Strain the liquid and discard. Store the peanuts in the refrigerator for up to a week.

Chive Oil

This adds not only a nice color, but also a nice punch of oil flavor. Use in Celery Root Bisque Salad (page 50) or just drizzle when you need a little sumthin' sumthin'.

◆ **Makes 1 cup (237 ml)** ◆

4-oz (113-g) bunch chives
1 cup (237 ml) blended oil
1 tsp salt

Blanch the chives in boiling water for 5 seconds, then transfer immediately to an ice bath. Add the chives, blended oil and salt to a blender, and mix on high for about 3 minutes. Strain and pour the oil in a small bowl or squeeze bottle. This will keep for a few days.

*See photo on right.

Neutral Vinaigrette

This is a very simple, across-the-board vinaigrette that will last forever and has a variety of uses other than just as a salad dressing. You can use this to dress up some vegetables, give some fish some added flavor, coat a pasta salad or even create a quick base for a marinade.

◆ **Makes about 2½ cups (593 ml)** ◆

½ cup (118 ml) white wine vinegar
1 tbsp (15 ml) Dijon mustard
1 cup (237 ml) extra-virgin olive oil
1 cup (237 ml) blended oil
Salt and pepper, to taste

Mix the white wine vinegar and Dijon mustard together. Then slowly whisk in both oils to emulsify. Season with salt and pepper. This dressing will keep for a month in the refrigerator.

Honey Butter

This is my favorite butter to finish something with. Whether brushing the tops of biscuits or drizzling on a chicken breast before slicing or even rubbing on an ear of corn, this stuff is delish!

◆ **Makes about 2 cups (454 g)** ◆

1 cup (227 g) unsalted butter
1 cup (237 ml) honey
1 tbsp (10 g) garlic powder

Melt the butter, honey and garlic powder together. This will keep for at least 2 weeks in the refrigerator.

SMOKED CINNAMON BUTTER

Everybody has had a cinnamon butter in their day, but this one is a touch unique because of the smoked cinnamon and agave syrup. This is great on sweet potatoes, a warm dessert or some really good bread. Try this on Buttermilk & Bourbon's Honey-Glazed Biscuits (page 13) and you will weep while you chew, it's so good.

◆ ══ **MAKES ABOUT 3 CUPS (688 G)** ══ ◆

1 cup (227 g) unsalted butter, room temperature

1 cup (125 g) powdered sugar

½ cup (118 ml) honey

½ cup (118 ml) agave

2 tsp (5 g) smoked cinnamon

Whip the butter, powdered sugar, honey, agave and smoked cinnamon in a stand mixer until very smooth. This will keep for at least 2 weeks in the refrigerator.

BUTTERMILK RANCH

Ranch dressing is good, but house-made buttermilk ranch is epic. Use this as a dipping sauce for some raw veggies or as a salad dressing or drizzle it over your fried chicken.

2 cups (475 ml) mayonnaise

1 cup (237 ml) buttermilk

2 tbsp (30 ml) red wine vinegar

2 tbsp (8 g) minced parsley

2 tbsp (6 g) minced chives

2 tbsp (1 g) minced fresh dill

1 tsp garlic powder

2 tbsp (14 g) onion powder

2 tbsp (13 g) celery salt

Pinch of cayenne

Salt and pepper, to taste

Whisk together the mayonnaise, buttermilk, vinegar, parsley, chives, dill, garlic powder, onion powder, celery salt and cayenne, then season with salt and pepper. This will keep refrigerated for a week.

Smoky Ham Stock

Smoked ham stock is the best. Try using it in place of chicken and see what happens. Great added flavor and a nice taste of the South.

◆ Makes about 1 gallon (3.75 L) ◆

3 smoked ham hocks

2 onions, peeled and cut in large chunks

1 cup (128 g) carrots, peeled and cut in large chunks

1 cup (100 g) roughly chopped celery

1 bunch scallions

4 cloves garlic

3 bay leaves

3 sprigs thyme

1 tbsp (10 g) black peppercorns

1½ gallons (5.6 L) water

Combine the ham hocks, onions, carrots, celery, scallions, garlic, bay leaves, thyme and peppercorns in a stockpot. Add the water and bring to a boil, then simmer for 4 hours, skimming off as much of the fat and scum as you can.

Once done, carefully strain the stock through a fine sieve into another pot. Use the stock immediately, or if you plan on storing it, place the pot in a sink full of ice water and stir to cool down the stock. Cover and refrigerate for up to 1 week or freeze.

Natural Chicken Stock

Cooks use chicken stock like Bob Ross uses paint. How was that analogy? Okay, moving on . . .
It's the staples of all staples. I like using the whole chicken because when I am done I can use the meat, and I feel like the meat helps add another layer of flavor. Duh.

◆ **Makes 2 quarts (2 L)** ◆

3 lbs (1.3 kg) natural chicken bones (or a whole natural chicken about 3½ lbs [1.5 kg], giblets removed)

2 carrots, cut in large chunks

3 stalks celery, cut in large chunks

2 onions, quartered

½ cup (67 g) garlic cloves

1 Granny Smith apple, halved

6 sprigs fresh thyme

1 sprig rosemary

2 bay leaves

1 bunch parsley

1 tsp whole black peppercorns

Place the chicken, carrots, celery, onions, garlic, apple, thyme, rosemary, bay leaves, parsley and peppercorns in a large stockpot over medium heat. Pour in only enough cold water to cover (about 3 quarts [3 L]). Allow it to slowly come to a boil. Lower the heat to a simmer and cook for 1½ to 2 hours. As it cooks, skim any impurities that rise to the surface; add a little more water if necessary to keep the ingredients covered while simmering.

Once done, carefully strain the stock through a fine sieve into another pot. Use the stock immediately, or if you plan on storing it, place the pot in a sink full of ice water and stir to cool down the stock. Cover and refrigerate for up to 1 week or freeze.

Vegetable Stock

Don't underestimate this recipe. We probably use this more than anything else in our kitchen. It's great for thinning out a sauce or puree or even a vinaigrette. It's better than using water and just adds a touch of flavor so it doesn't interfere with the recipe. Keep this around and you won't believe how much you use it.

◆ **Makes 2 quarts (2 L)** ◆

2 onions, peeled and cut in large chunks

1 Granny Smith apple, cut in large chunks

2 stalks celery, cut in large chunks

4 carrots, peeled and cut in large chunks

½ cup (67 g) garlic cloves

2 bay leaves

1 tsp fennel seeds

1 tsp black peppercorns

1 bunch parsley

In a large pot, combine the onions, apple, celery, carrots, garlic, bay leaves, fennel seeds, peppercorns and parsley and add water to cover by at least 2 inches (5 cm). Bring to a boil, then shut off the heat and let it sit for an hour.

Once done, carefully strain the stock through a fine sieve into another pot. Use the stock immediately, or if you plan on storing it, place the pot in a sink full of ice water and stir to cool down the stock. Cover and refrigerate for up to 1 week or freeze.

LOBSTER STOCK

I have this weird fascination with making lobster stock. It has so much flavor and I don't know any home cook who makes it. Now you can, and I promise you it will elevate the flavor and richness of any recipe! Also, you can swap out shellfish shells such as mussels, crab or shrimp to change the flavor profile.

◆ ⬧ MAKES 2 QUARTS (2 L) ⬧ ◆

1 tbsp (15 ml) extra-virgin olive oil

Shells from 2 lobsters

1 onion, peeled and cut in large chunks

2 stalks celery, cut in large chunks

2 carrots, peeled and cut in large chunks

4 cloves garlic

1 tbsp (10 g) black peppercorns

4 sprigs thyme

6 bay leaves

2 cups (475 ml) dry white wine

1 (8-oz [227-g]) can diced tomatoes, drained

1 gallon (3.75 L) water

Heat the olive oil in a large pot. When the oil is hot, add the lobster shells and cook until they are bright red and almost caramelized looking, about 10 to 15 minutes (this is very important in order to get a deep, rich stock). Add the onion, celery and carrots and cook for 5 minutes, until the vegetables start to brown. Add the garlic, peppercorns, thyme, bay leaves, wine, tomatoes and water and simmer for 1 hour.

Once done, carefully strain the stock through a fine sieve into another pot. Use the stock immediately, or if you plan on storing it, place the pot in a sink full of ice water and stir to cool down the stock. Cover and refrigerate for up to 1 week or freeze.

Refried Red Beans

This is the very back of the book, but this is ironically one of my favorite recipes in this book. It doesn't necessarily go with anything in particular, but this is amazing stuff. You can absolutely serve this as just as an accompaniment with chicken or pork or something else, but after you taste how good this is, you will figure what that "something else" is.

Serves 6 to 8

2 cups (300 g) diced Spanish onion

¼ cup (34 g) garlic, minced

1 cup (204 g) lard

3 (15-oz [425-g]) cans red beans, drained and rinsed

2 tsp (5 g) House Cajun Spice (page 155)

Salt and pepper, to taste

¼ cup (25 g) sliced scallions, for garnish

In a heavy-bottomed pot, sauté the onion and garlic in the lard until soft. Add the red beans and House Cajun Spice and cook until the beans are very soft, about 10 minutes. Remove half of the mixture and puree it, and then fold it back in. Season with salt and pepper and garnish with scallions.

Garlic Confit

The old way of making roasted garlic is dead to you and me. This new recipe is faster, easier and will give you virtually the same product.

2 cups (475 ml) extra-virgin olive oil

2 cups (268 g) garlic cloves, peeled

Heat the olive oil in a small saucepan over medium-low heat. Add the garlic; cook over very low heat about 30 minutes, until the garlic is soft and tender and slightly brown, but not falling apart.

Transfer the garlic with a slotted spoon to a clean jar, and pour the oil in to cover the cloves. Cool the mixture to room temperature. Cover the jar tightly and keep refrigerated for several weeks.

Acknowledgments

To my wife, Thuy, thank you for loving me unconditionally, being so supportive, being my toughest critic and keeping me grounded. Thank you for always pushing me to grow. Also, for taking me to New Orleans that one day—it has changed our life. I love you.

To my mom, I honestly don't even know where to begin other than to just say thank you for your unconditional love, guidance and just always being there for me. Without you and what you have done for me my whole life, I would absolutely not be where I am today.

To my dad, Victor, I miss you and wish you were here to see this, but I think you would be very proud of this book even though there are a lot of chicken recipes in it.

To my Jill, Steve, John and Maureen, thank you for being my number one fans and always believing in me.

To the Le family, thank you for supporting me and my restaurants every day and for being great friends and family.

To Jack and Billy, thank you for all the opportunities you have given me over the years, trusting me with your money and helping me get the restaurant started and for all your endless advice.

To my publicist, Nicole, pretty positive I would not be even close to where I am today without all your hard work, dedication and passive-aggressive ways of forcing me to do all those interviews over the years. Thank you for believing in me even when others may not have.

To my business partners, thank you for helping me grow and for trusting me and my food.

To Jeff, thank you for all your dedication and your relentless hard work. Thank you for helping me develop and test all these recipes and being my right hand from day one. 1,000 percent could not and would not have done this without you.

To my friend, manager, driver, agent, life coach, barista, etc., Pablo, thank you for always believing in the Jason Santos brand and working so hard to help me further my career with little gratification on your end. One day we will have coconuts!

To Ken Goodman, thank you for truly capturing the essence of my food and my personality with your stunning photos and dealing with my OCD during our shoot. And for not making me go to Maryland for a backdrop.

To Colleen, thank you for dealing with me over the years and my sometimes difficult ways and for all your hard work and creativity. I couldn't have done it without you.

To all my chefs and restaurant managers, thank you for all your devotion and your hard work day after day. Thank you for being patient with me. I know it can be hard.

To Page Street Publishing, thank you for making this such an easy process and for putting your trust in me to produce a great book.

To C3 Entertainment, thank you for believing in me when some people would not have and spending countless hours working on helping me develop my brand.

To Erica Diskin, thanks for your design vision and for making everything come to fruition.

ABOUT THE AUTHOR

One of Boston's most creative and charismatic chefs, the blue-haired Jason Santos has wowed guests with his innovative cuisine and his larger-than-life personality at his 3 bustling restaurants: Buttermilk & Bourbon, Citrus & Salt and Abby Lane.

While other kids grew up watching Sesame Street, Chef Jason Santos grew up experimenting in his grandmother's kitchen and watching, and idolizing, Julia Child. It was during his early years spent in the kitchen that Santos realized his passion for cooking—a passion he would spend the rest of his life cultivating.

After graduating from Newbury College's culinary arts program in Newton, Massachusetts, at age 19, Santos began his culinary career at Chris Schlesinger's The Blue Room and then moved on to Andy Husbands's Boston institution Tremont 647, where he spent six years honing his personal style and rising through the ranks to executive chef. In 2005, Santos accepted the executive chef position at Gargoyles on the Square in Somerville's Davis Square neighborhood. While at Gargoyles on the Square, Santos's innovative cuisine transformed the restaurant from neighborhood stalwart to out-of-town dining destination while winning many accolades.

Following his success in Boston's best kitchens, Santos competed on Season 7 of FOX's hit television show *Hell's Kitchen*. Santos's larger-than-life personality and culinary expertise quickly positioned him as a fan favorite and garnered the attention of one of the industry's top critics, Chef Gordon Ramsay. His successful run on the show concluded with a runner-up finish and a newfound national recognition.

After *Hell's Kitchen* wrapped, Santos returned to Boston to add "restaurateur" to his growing résumé. In the summer of 2013, he opened his first restaurant. Within the next five years, Santos opened two more Boston mainstays.

Santos now divides his time as owner and executive chef at Abby Lane, a sleek, two-floor restaurant located in the heart of Boston's Theater District; Buttermilk & Bourbon, a Southern-inspired restaurant that offers a taste of Southern hospitality in the heart of the city; and Citrus & Salt, a coastal Mexican restaurant in the Back Bay. Santos's cuisine seamlessly combines Mexican, French, Southern and traditional American flavors—often incorporating molecular gastronomy techniques to create dazzling dishes as inventive as they are delicious.

Santos is also a recurring guest on the *Today* show, CBS's *Early Show*, the CBS television show *The Talk* and subsequent seasons of *Hell's Kitchen*. Santos also currently appears on the Paramount Network's *Bar Rescue*, rehabilitating failing restaurants and bars as a chef expert alongside Jon Taffer.

Despite balancing three lively restaurants and filming, Santos donates his time to Share Our Strength's No Kid Hungry, an organization dedicated to ending childhood hunger and with which he has been involved for 22 years.

INDEX